FIVE STAR Change

★ ★ ★ ★ ★

Facilitating Transitions Effectively

Alan E. Nelson, Ed.D.

Copyright 2020

Alan E. Nelson

Summit Publishing
235A Moorpark Rd.
Ste. 1622
Thousand Oaks, CA 91358

ISBN: 9781661808198

acknowledgements

- Thanks to the many thought leaders I've learned from, on what causes humans to reject and accept new ideas.
- Thanks to my graduate and undergraduate students who've put up with my teaching over the years and encouraged me to further the change model, explained in this book.
- Thanks to Evelyn Torres for the wonderful graphics that reinforce the concepts.
- Thanks to Karen Kluever for the stellar editing.
- Thanks to Jeff White for his branding expertise and cover formatting.
- Thanks to change-agent models I've observed firsthand and consider friends: Bob Hunt, Mike Ingram, Jeff DeWit, Jay Johnson, Thom and Joni Schultz.
- Thanks to my dad and mom, who invested so much in me. My mother's transition from this world still impacts me. I miss you, Mom.
- Thanks as always to my wife of nearly 40 years, Nancy, who's responded like a star to the ups and downs of my transitions through life. She's my best friend, Mom to our three great sons (Jeff, Josh and Jesse) and Nanna to our sublime granddaughters (Juniper and Ivy).

a message from the author

Throughout my life, I've been a student of leadership, whether as a leader myself, a professor of leadership and organizational behavior, or a back-row participant. The primary life work of a leader is to assist people through change processes, whether it's Moses convincing his followers to seek a new land or Steve Jobs reviving Apple. Yet research shows that a majority of these projects fail. The reason isn't so much flawed ideas, but rather an inability of those in charge to understand how difficult it is for people to let go of the familiar.

This book is a distillation of over 30 years of reviewing the literature, plus observing and interacting with scores of leaders about effective and ineffective improvement efforts. It will show you how to create a visual graphic that depicts the influencers in your change efforts. You'll learn how to compute a simple, numerical index to estimate the psychological resistance, based on four key factors. Plus, you'll discover ways to design a transition plan to improve the likelihood of a smooth transition. It's designed to empower those who want to improve the performance and quality of their teams, companies, nonprofits, and organizations, by creating a better transition experience. I hope you find this book a benefit. I believe you will.

Alan E. Nelson

Los Angeles

chapter one

"Metcalf party of four," the golf course manager called.

"Okay, you all ready?" Ben said, motioning to the first tee box. "We're up."

Ben slid onto the golf cart seat beside his supervisor, Sarah Wembly, senior vice president of their company. He enjoyed their quarterly outings. Sarah gathered her three VPs for an afternoon of socializing and casual business talk. He, Jaime, and Nicole got along well. Each received a lot of autonomy, and their divisions operated in significantly different markets.

"How's your family?" Sarah asked, holding onto the edge of the roof, as Ben pushed on the accelerator.

"Oh, they're great," Ben said, smiling brightly. "It's pretty crazy with two kids in school and sports, but I wouldn't miss it for the world."

"How's Beth doing with her new home business?"

"She's loving it. No commute. Technology is amazing," Ben responded. "We try to trade off getting the kids ready in the morning, but I'll be honest, she's the superior parent."

"I'm so glad the home office transition went well," Sarah responded.

"Thanks for asking."

Ben and Sarah arrived at the first tee, followed by Jaime and Nicole in their cart. The previous foursome was still finishing their drives, as Ben locked the brake. "Looks like they called us a bit early or we're just fast," Ben said.

"No problem. We're not in a rush," Sarah reassured. "How's the new strategic initiative looking in your division?"

Ben wasn't sure how to respond to Sarah's question. He didn't want to convey his concerns, since he wanted to make a good impression. Yet, he knew he couldn't bluff Sarah, given her knowledge and experience.

"Oh, you know, we're heading into some turbulent waters as we approach the big change," he said. "I'm still trying to get my head around how we'll sell it to our management team. It's a pretty significant difference from how we've worked in the past."

"That it is," Sarah said, affirmingly. "I've been thinking about you and what you're going to be facing the next couple of years."

"Keeping my fingers crossed," Ben said, grinning sheepishly.

"Well, I'm all for luck, but if you're open to it, I'd like to connect you with an old consultant friend of mine. We call him The Catalyst."

Ben chuckled. "The Catalyst? Sounds like change is right down his alley."

"Yeah, he's sort of a guru in the field. All I know is that he saved my bacon a few years ago, when we were white-knuckling it during the recession. We probably wouldn't have survived, given the changes we needed to make. He taught me about Five-Star Change." Sarah got out of the cart and stood beside her bag of clubs.

"Hey, I'm certainly open to ideas," Ben responded. "Looks like it paid off. You got a pretty big promotion."

Sarah chuckled. "That's true. I did. I don't know if he's taking any new clients or even if he's still consulting, but if you could spend a little time with him, I know you'd enjoy it. He won't tell you what to do, but he'll certainly give you some tools for fixing what we both think needs to happen in your division."

"Why do you call him The Catalyst?" Ben asked.

Sarah paused. "I'm not really sure. The person who recommended him to me called him that. I guess it's what he does best, helps organizations change. He helped us avoid making some bad mistakes. I think you'll like him."

"Where's he located?"

"He lives north of LA, so if he can't come to you, perhaps you can go to him." Sarah looked up at the tee box where Nicole and Jaime were waiting.

"You two want to golf or talk shop?" Jaime called, smiling at Ben and Sarah.

"Guess we better get to it," she said, pulling a driver out of her bag.

The afternoon on the course was enjoyable with collegial work conversation, punctuated by golf jokes and teasing. Ben hoped he could do a better job keeping the upcoming changes on target, than some of his shots. His boss's offer seemed intriguing, but in the back of his mind, he wondered if she sensed something he didn't. The timing seemed impeccable. Little did Ben suspect how his upcoming connection with the change expert would transform the way he led, not just his upcoming initiative.

chapter two

    A couple weeks passed since Ben and his supervisor spent the afternoon on the golf course. Sure enough, Sarah delivered on her commitment to connect him with her former advisor, whom she referred to as The Catalyst. The two men lined up an initial meeting at his home office.

    As Ben drove from his company's offices in downtown Los Angeles, he wondered if he could be using his time better. Despite his boss's recommendation to connect with her past consultant, he felt he should be putting in more time developing the strategic plan. The large-scale restructuring idea made sense to him and had the support of Sarah and others further up the food chain, but he wasn't sure how the rest in his division would respond. It would likely mean a change of roles, practices, and, for a few, employment.

Ben exited the 101 freeway and headed toward a nearby neighborhood. After a couple of turns, he stopped at a vine-covered security gate call box. Ben punched in the number. The phone rang. "I'll beep you in," a voice said. "Just drive forward, and you'll see visitor parking on the right." Slowly, the black, wrought iron gates opened. Ben drove forward and pulled into a slot.

As Ben pulled his sports jacket off of the hook, a voice behind him got his attention.

"You won't need that," an older man said, standing behind the car. "You must be Ben." He reached out his hand and Ben shook it.

"You must be The Catalyst," Ben said, grinning. "It's good to meet you."

The older man laughed. "That's what some call me," he said. "It's not a moniker I sought, but I guess it stuck, so it's what I answer to these days." He chuckled again.

Ben closed the back door of his car, leaving his jacket on the hook.

"Thanks for driving up," The Catalyst said. "I don't do a lot of consulting these days, but when I do, I try to telecommute by video. But it's kind of nice having a face-to-face with someone local."

"I really appreciate the time," Ben answered. "Sarah has great things to say about you."

The Catalyst chuckled. "Well, she said good things about you, too. Your supervisor is an amazing leader."

"She is," Ben affirmed.

"Let's go up to my office," the man said, pointing. Ben followed his host through the front door of a townhome and up a staircase to an office. "This is where I hang out these days," he said. "Here's some water." He fetched a bottle from a small, white refrigerator, handing it to Ben.

Ben looked around the room, noticing a plaque of a former US president, some Asian décor, and an exercise bike. He walked over to a wall bookcase beside the desk and started reading the titles on the shelves.

"Ah, you're a reader," The Catalyst remarked. "I like to see what leaders have on their bookshelves, too. You can tell a lot about a person that way."

Ben smiled in response, noticing shelves of books referencing change.

"Let me introduce you to some of my favorites," The Catalyst offered. "Here are some classics." He pulled a book off the shelf and handed it to Ben. "*Leading Change* by John Kotter is a bestseller. His sequel, *A Sense of Urgency*, is also great. Kotter is a legend."

"I started reading *Leading Change* awhile back," Ben admitted. "I should finish it."

"Here's another one," The Catalyst said, handing Ben a hardback book with a blue cover. "*Deep Change* by Robert Quinn. You'll love this book."

Just as Ben began reading the back of the Quinn book, the consultant handed him another. "Here's my personal favorite, *Managing Transitions*, by Bridges. I heard William speak years ago. His passion was about helping people manage life transitions, not just in organizations. At the end of the day, it's all about changes in life, isn't it?"

"That's right," Ben said, scanning the cover of the book.

"Bridges passed away several years ago. He lived just north of San Francisco," The Catalyst said, appearing to know the author on a personal basis. "Ah, and what would change be without *Who Moved My Cheese?* and *Our Iceberg is Melting*?"

The Catalyst placed two small paperbacks on the desk in front of Ben. These introduced the change process on a mass scale by using the power of story.

"With so many books written on change, why aren't we better at it?"

The Catalyst sat down, leaned back in his chair and laughed. "That's the million-dollar question. I guess the best answer is that we as humans don't always learn well. Someone said, history doesn't repeat itself; people repeat history. We tend to replicate what we've seen. In this case, we don't take change seriously. Those in charge assume their colleagues and employees will embrace innovation and new ideas, but most do not. Then they try to force change and it comes back to bite them. They are well-intended, but ignorant. I don't mean that in a deprecating way, but in the literal sense. The word ignorant is from the Latin *ignorare*, to refuse to take notice, to shut your eyes. They're not stupid. They just don't know what they don't know."

"Why do people resist change so much?" Ben asked.

"Please, have a seat," The Catalyst said, gesturing toward a chair on the opposite side of the desk. "According to Kotter, a former Harvard professor, around 70% of change endeavors fail."

"Wow, that's a lot," Ben responded. "Why so many?"

"There are a lot of theories. Kotter blames much of it on lacking a sense of urgency. I also agree with William Bridges that a lot of it has to do with people's wiring in general."

"What do you mean?" Ben asked, taking a swig of water.

"Well, I find it interesting that some experts suggest around 70% of people tend to have an aversion to change. Their temperament prefers the status quo and they don't necessarily enjoy trying new things. At the same time, other psychologists say that around 70% of people possess an external locus of control."

"What's that?" Ben asked.

"Locus of control refers to our perception of how much control we have over the events in our lives, such as our happiness and well-being. An individual with an internal locus of control believes you can somewhat determine your fate, that regardless of circumstances and external factors, you can make good things happen. The problem is that less than a third of people are wired this way. Think about it. When you stand in line at Starbucks and hear people complaining about the weather, stock market, or any number of other things. Someone asks, 'How are you doing?' and the person says, 'Not bad, under the circumstances.' Well, what are you doing under there?"

Ben chuckled.

"An external locus of control reflects an attitude that things in the environment control our well-being. An internal locus of control believes that a person, not the conditions, contains more influence. Nearly all leaders possess an internal locus of control. A common quality is that they believe they can improve things. They are, as Napoleon said, 'purveyors of hope.'"

Ben thought about The Catalyst's comments. "Mind if I take some notes?"

"I'd be disappointed if you didn't." Ben opened his portfolio and began writing.

"Any ideas of why so many people are wired as change averse?"

"My hunch is that, by nature, we're creatures of habit. In social psychology, they discovered a phenomenon called the *mere-exposure effect*. It shows that people tend to develop a preference for things, merely because they are familiar with them. Familiarity reduces stress. It's a survival thing. We resort to what is known and comfortable, so we perpetuate the status quo. Change, therefore, has the potential to threaten our well-being, whether it's an opponent, a saber-toothed tiger attacking us, or inclement weather. Leaders need to understand this if they want to help their people transition."

"By transition, do you mean change?"

The Catalyst leaned back in his chair and smiled. "Good catch. I like that. Transition is actually different than change. William Bridges notes that change is what happens externally, physically. Transition is what happens internally, emotionally, psychologically."

Ben wrote more notes. He looked up, pausing to clarify his thoughts. "So, you're saying that change projects don't happen, primarily because leaders don't help people transition well."

The Catalyst smiled and touched his nose. "Bingo, you got it. Most business people are trained to think in terms of improvement plans, what needs to be done better. But an improvement plan is different from a transition plan. You need both, but they're different."

The Catalyst leaned down, opened a drawer, and pulled out a pad of paper. He took a felt tip pen out of a green, marble holder on his desk and drew a line down the middle of the page. On the left side at the top, he wrote "Improvement" and on the right side "Transition."

"The bolder ink will help us see this better," The Catalyst said. He then added, "where we're going" in the left column and then "where we're now" in the right. "An improvement plan is about where we want to be, the goal, objective, and finish line. A transition plan focuses on where we are now, because the distance between where you are and where you want to go will determine how you develop your strategy."

"What do you mean?"

"Look at the popular, high-tech companies in Silicon Valley," The Catalyst said. "When you start from scratch, you don't have years of traditions or culture to fight. Companies with a legacy behind them start from a different location than an organization that is young and agile. Culture is highly elastic. It returns to its original position, when you stop applying concerted effort. The distance between where you are and where you want to be impacts your plan. A transition plan looks at that."

Ben silently processed The Catalyst's comments, jotting notes on his notepad. The Catalyst opened the top drawer of his desk and pulled out a rubber band. "Look. Let's say my left hand represents where we want to go. We want to be like XYZ company." He stretched the rubber band upward with his left hand. "My right hand represents where we are now. Let's say that XYZ company was here, where my right hand is. But what if our company is here?" The Catalyst pulled the rubber band down with his right hand. "As you can see, we have a lot more distance to gain than XYZ company, if we want to get where they are. Thus, a transition plan focuses on the current location, not just the anticipated destination."

"That makes sense," Ben said.

The consultant started writing again. In the Improvement column, he wrote, "resources/structure" and under the transition side, "people/culture." He said, "An improvement plan focuses on resources, such as money, personnel, and organizational structure. A transition plan looks at the people, in terms of how they're wired, and then culture, how flexible and responsive it is. Both are important, but they're quite different."

Ben continued jotting notes. The Catalyst wrote more words, then said, "An improvement plan uses 'logic, targeting the mind,' whereas a transition plan aims at the 'heart and feelings.' Thus, an improvement plan tends to focus on the left hemisphere of the brain that is 'analytical and methodical.' A transition plan is more right-brained, emphasizing 'imagination and artistry.'"

The Catalyst continued. "An improvement plan focuses on 'know-how and talents,' whereas a transition plan looks at 'relationships and influence.' Granted, these are all important, but quite different. An improvement plan needs 'risk and boldness,' while a transition plan includes 'patience and perseverance.'"

Ben wrote his notes and then looked up. "I'm not sure I understand. Wouldn't a transition plan require risk and boldness, too?"

"Actually, because a significant improvement plan will be risky and bold, leaders need to think in terms of the social and emotional responses of their people. That means they'll need to be extra patient and make sure they don't quit when things become difficult, as they probably will. They'll need to persist."

The two men sat in silence, as Ben processed the ideas.

The Catalyst began writing again. "At the end of the day, an improvement plan is more 'managerial and strategic,'" he said. "A transition plan is about 'leadership and vision.' It's what leaders do, initiate change within people, not just the organization. Improvement is about what needs to happen. Transition focuses on how we're going to implement it." Turning the notes toward Ben, who was copying them, he said, "Obviously, both plans are needed, but since business people are trained to think improvement versus transition, they tend to err in the latter."

Ben finished writing and then looked up. "Wow, I can see from the right column how much more challenging this is than the left side."

IMPROVEMENT	TRANSITION
- where we're going	- where we're now
- resources/structure	- people/culture
- logic/mind (left)	- heart/feelings (right)
- know-how/talents	- relationships/influence
- risk/boldness	- patience/perseverance
- managerial/strategic	- leadership/vision

"Soft skills are hard," The Catalyst affirmed. "It's why there's such a shortage of Five-Star Changes."

The two men continued to talk. They agreed to meet again in the next two weeks, after Ben had a chance to process what they'd discussed and think more about developing a transition plan. What he didn't realize is that he would also discover why his boss referred to The Catalyst's work as Five-Star Change.

> Meeting Notes:
> - Over 2/3 of significant change efforts fail
> - Over 2/3 of people have an external locus of control; focus on environment
> - Leaders have an internal locus of control; believe they can change things
> - Change is external; transition is internal
> - An improvement plan differs from a transition plan

FIVE STAR CHANGE

chapter three

The drive up the 101 freeway gave Ben an opportunity to think about his meeting with The Catalyst. He thought a lot about their conversation a week ago that incubated several ideas. As soon as he saw the Lindero Canyon exit sign, he got in the right lane. For some reason, the consultant wanted to meet at the Four Seasons Hotel, just off the 101. Ben pulled his car around to the front and handed his keys to the valet, taking the card receipt. He noticed a Bentley, Rolls Royce, and a high-end BMW, backed in, just to the right of the main door. He smiled to himself, "Not your typical neighborhood." The doorman greeted him as did another staff member in the lobby, who also offered assistance. Ben graciously declined, looking around for his guest.

"Hey, there you are," a familiar voice called. "Welcome to the Four Seasons, Ben."

"Good morning and thank you," Ben said, shaking hands with his coach or consultant. He wasn't quite sure what to call him yet. Referring to him as The Catalyst seemed so eccentric.

"I thought it might be nice for us to meet here, since it's right off the freeway and a few minutes closer to you than my house," The Catalyst explained. "Can I buy you a coffee?" he asked, pointing to a coffee shop named Stir, beside the lobby.

"No, but thank you," Ben said. "I had some on my way up."

"Let's take a little walk before we sit," The Catalyst said, motioning Ben to join him in the hall. The two men walked through the luxury hotel corridor, past a light and bright restaurant named Coin and Candor, followed by a sleek-looking, Japanese cuisine eatery called ONYX. "Beautiful, isn't it? This Four Seasons is owned by a billionaire named David Murdock. He's a real estate tycoon who also owns Dole, the fruit company. Dole used to have its headquarters across from the entrance, but not long ago it relocated, and the Hilton Foundation took over that building. Let's head this way," The Catalyst said, retracing their steps in the opposite direction.

The two walked past an attractive-looking pub and then a kitchen. "They offer culinary classes there." Ben paused to look inside. "Pretty cool, eh?" The Catalyst commented. The pair continued into a grand foyer with a water feature and tall, stone artwork in the middle.

"Wow, what is this?" Ben asked.

"This wing is called the California Health and Longevity Institute. It includes a spa, workout facility, and a staff of doctors who help people get in shape and stay healthy."

"Impressive."

"Let's go upstairs. They have a lounge area where we can talk, called the Library."

The Catalyst led Ben to a room, lined with dark wooden shelves, filled with books. The two sat across from each other in wing-backed chairs.

"Thanks again for driving up," The Catalyst said. "I don't have a lot of time these days, between staying busy with my clients and pursuing semi-retirement."

"We should probably talk about fees," Ben said, pulling out his notepad.

"We probably should," The Catalyst responded. "This series is on me. As long as you're willing to drive and our schedule works out, it's complimentary, based on my work with Sarah in the past. If we need to ramp up things down the road, we can go there, but for now my goal is to load you up with best practices about effective transitions."

"Wow, that's very generous. I really appreciate this," Ben said, sincerely.

"You're welcome. The last time we met, I mentioned that over two-thirds of change efforts fail. If that many don't succeed, you can assume that a lot of improvement plans that get adopted only do so with a good amount of kicking and screaming." The Catalyst continued, "Look around you. This hotel is rated five stars. It's five-star service, five-star food, five-star amenities, and five-star beauty. I don't want you to be happy with two-, three-, or even four-star transitions. Your goal is to pursue Five-Star Change."

Ben jotted notes. "Sarah mentioned that phrase when she first spoke of you." He paused and looked up. "No doubt, this is a gorgeous hotel and facility, but if this is your standard for organizational change, why invest so much into luxury, when something less would suffice? Is Five-Star practical?"

"Here's why," The Catalyst said, leaning forward. "Whenever you experience less than Five-Star Change, you diminish the trust of others and condition people to fear change.

It's Pavlovian. The more we experience crappy innovation processes, we begin to loathe anything other than the status quo. It's operant conditioning. If I get a shock every time I put my hand on a metal bar, I'll stop touching that bar. But if I get a treat whenever I touch the bar, I'll be tapping it a lot."

"So, you're saying that one reason change is difficult is because people have had such bad experiences with it."

"That's right," The Catalyst affirmed. "Mark Twain said that after a cat sits on a hot stove once, he won't sit on it again. Of course, the cat won't sit on a cold stove either. Every bad transition experience conditions people to be change averse. The reason why Five-Star Change is so important is because change needs to happen more and more as technology and society evolve. But when leaders fail to make transitions a positive, healthy process, people resist it. And when leaders decrease trust, their ability to lead goes down, because trust is the currency of leading. We won't follow who we don't trust. We certainly won't sacrifice for them. That's why turnover goes up, commitment goes down, and leaders tend to leave, when they fail to facilitate change effectively."

Ben nodded his head, thinking about The Catalyst's words. He continued writing notes.

"What if it's the wrong thing, meaning it's a flawed innovation?"

"What do you mean?"

"I mean, what if you transition a new idea brilliantly, but it's the wrong idea?"

The Catalyst laughed. "Great point. A Five-Star Change process won't turn a flawed idea into a good one. That goes back to our first discussion. An improvement plan is different from a transition plan, but you need both. The idea has to be a good one. It must solve a problem. Research shows that the two things people look for most in leaders are competence and compassion. People want to sense that you know what you're doing and that you care about them. Fail with either one and you'll be a less effective leader or not a leader at all.

"But, here's the bigger problem. When we try to implement an excellent idea ineffectively, people and organizations end up rejecting what will make things better. This is the plight of far more organizations than effectively adopting inept innovations."

Ben paused, letting the ideas marinate in his mind.

"Let me say this another way," The Catalyst continued. "Leaders tend to be far more effective at coming up with good ideas than they are at getting others to adopt them. The primary reason is that they're trained in planning, not transitioning. They strategize solutions versus people. Coming up with great ideas isn't as difficult as getting others to embrace them. The first requires critical thinking. It's a logical process, but the latter is about influencing and motivating people. As I said last time, one is a left-brained process and the other right brained. Soft skills are often elusive. It's about understanding how people are wired, how they emote, and what motivates them."

"That makes sense," Ben said, leaning back in his chair.

"Alright, let's talk about the people you need to transition. Let me give you some home work," The Catalyst said. "This is what we'll need to create an Influence Constellation, the first component of a change model I'm going to teach you."

"What's an Influence Constellation?"

"An Influence Constellation is a visual presentation that graphically plots where the Opinion Leaders are in terms of how they feel and think about the new idea you're proposing, the improvement."

"How do you define an Opinion Leader?"

"Let's talk politics," The Catalyst said. "The word politics is rooted in the Greek word *polis*, meaning city. In essence, it's about people in community. Wherever you have relationships, there will be politics, so while we sometimes think of it negatively, it's simply about people relating to each other. It can be good and it can be bad."

"That makes sense," Ben affirmed.

"So, let's talk about Opinion Leaders. What do you think I mean by that term?"

"They are people with influence; they're people who can make things happen or stop progress," Ben answered.

"Spot on," The Catalyst said. "Opinion Leaders don't necessarily have a title or even an official vote, but others listen to their thoughts and opinions. I like to think of it in terms of thermostats and thermometers. A thermometer tells the temperature, but a thermostat sets the temperature. Opinion Leaders are the thermostats."

"Ooh, I like that," Ben said, writing down the metaphor.

"Sometimes, people confuse influencers with people who talk a lot, but they don't necessarily dominate airtime. They do get listened to the most. They're often the ones who are asked questions, and people physically face or look at them during discussions. Peers rely on them for their opinions, before a vote or prior to making a decision."

"So, what if you have a person who has a vote, but doesn't really have much influence?"

"Good question, because that frequently happens. A vote might result from a position, such as a person who oversees a budget or must sign off on a plan. In an authority structure, you need to include that person, but only if he or she can approve or stop a suggested change. More importantly, you need to consider those who may not have a title or official role, but whose opinion has impact. This is informal influence."

"What's the difference between power and influence?"

"I think they're pretty much the same, although those who study organizational behavior tend to define power as the potential to influence, whereas influence is power activated," The Catalyst explained.

"Hmm," Ben muttered, taking notes.

"I know our time today has been brief, but before we meet next time, I'd like you to come up with a list of the six to ten most influential people in your division, who could make this new change plan a great process or who could make it difficult or even shut it down."

"Okay, so we're talking about specific individuals, not groups, right?"

"Exactly. In fact, you're not that interested in the larger group's opinion. People take their cues from Opinion Leaders in their identified social circles. History is not made by the masses. It's made by individuals who influence them. This is the social reality of leadership. The only time you want to do an organizational survey is to better understand the climate and perhaps determine how much marketing will help. This isn't a popularity contest or democratic vote. Simply identify the Opinion Leaders and find out where they stand. Then, you can predict the outcomes."

"That seems a lot more manageable."

"It is. When a leader makes decisions based on the results of opinion surveys, they're naïve and likely not a strong leader. Savvy leaders know that it's the Opinion Leaders who influence the masses. Focus on them, and they'll take care of the rest."

"Got it."

"The reason this is more strategic is because Opinion Leaders consist of less than 10% of the total. In society, the one to ten managerial ratio is dominant. On average, a manager oversees ten people or ten facilities. The person above that person oversees ten. The average span of control ratio is one to ten.

"So, your homework is to come up with a list of the six to ten strongest Opinion Leaders in your division, whose influence will cause others to accept or reject the change idea you're advocating. I also want you to think about how each person responds to change in general, the size of his or her influence, and what each person thinks specifically about the new idea you're planning. We'll use that information to create the Influence Constellation I mentioned, the next time we meet."

The two men talked more as they left the library, walking through the Four Seasons. Ben tipped the valet, thinking about the quality of the hotel. He wanted to facilitate Five-Star Change as a leader, but it wouldn't be until the next meeting that he'd uncover the politics of making that happen, as well as potential change assassins in his division.

Meeting Notes:
- Five-Star Change represents the best quality of transitions
- People fear change because they're conditioned by low quality transition experiences
- An effective transition process won't turn a bad improvement idea into a good one.
- Power is potential influence; influence is power activated
- Opinion Leaders (OL) are those who influence the attitudes of others, whether in official positions of authority or not
- A thermometer tells the temperature but a thermostat sets it; OLs are thermostats
- OLs represent 5 - 10% in an organization; identify and monitor them and you'll know how the rest will go

# FIVE STAR CHANGE

chapter four

Ben anticipated his meeting with The Catalyst this morning as he drove out of Los Angeles. In addition to the new ideas he gleaned, he enjoyed the consultant's demeanor and reassuring approach. Once again, Ben exited the 101 at Lindero Canyon Road, but this time he turned left, away from the Four Seasons Hotel. Turning right on Agoura Road, he looked at the plush golf course on his right and then pulled into the Westlake Village Inn, a low-profile hotel with a classic, Tuscany-style architecture. He parked and walked toward a winery and coffee shop called The Stonehaus. *The Catalyst schedules interesting venues for our meetings*, Ben thought.

As usual, The Catalyst arrived before his guest. As soon as he saw Ben walk in, he stood up from a table under a large, covered patio, dotted with customers. A small fountain gurgled in the middle, and a fire burned in the fireplace on the other side.

"Hey, welcome," the older gentleman said, greeting Ben with a handshake and then pulling him in for a hug. "Hope that's okay. You remind me of our sons."

Ben chuckled. "Absolutely, we're a hugging family, too. I was just thinking as I drove up how much I'm enjoying our times together. Thanks for investing in me."

"It's an honor," the older man responded. "Come, let me give you a little tour before we get to work."

"Sure," Ben said, following his host.

"Have you ever seen *The Bachelor* TV show?"

"I don't watch it, but we have friends who are big fans," Ben responded.

"Well, I don't know if you noticed, but you pulled into the Westlake Village Inn. Sometimes you'll see that at the start of the series, as some of the contestants stay there. The host, Chris Harrison, lives nearby and the mansion where they film is up Kanan Road. In fact, quite a few entertainment people live in this area, since it's near Hollywood, but a bit removed from the LA congestion."

The men sauntered past another, larger water fountain, through a tiny vineyard and then a grand, round fountain on the street corner.

"This is amazing," Ben said. "Do they actually use those grapes?"

"It's a working vineyard. You can buy wine made from grapes grown on those vines. People from all over come here. Believe it or not, this site was originally planned to be a gas station, but the owner had a much grander idea."

"It's much better than a gas station. Wow!"

"Good change always makes sense afterward, even if it's not easy."

The two walked back toward the café, ordered coffees, and sat down at a table beside the fireplace.

"What's on our agenda today?" Ben asked.

"Well, we have sort of a marathon meeting, which is why I asked you to come early and then we can work over lunch. I'm going to introduce you to a change model called NCM that I designed after years of reviewing the literature and interacting with scores of organizational leaders. The model has three components, an Influence Constellation, a four-factor formula, and then a Transition Index analysis, based on what the formula reveals. I'll explain the Influence Constellation in a little bit. First, let's look at your list of Opinion Leaders."

"Okay," Ben said, pulling a sheet of paper out of the pocket of his notepad.

"Let's see what you have." There were eight names on the list, along with titles or adjectives for each.

#	Name	Title
1.	Sarah	SVP
2.	John	Marketing Coordinator
3.	Julie	Sales Coordinator
4.	Michael	Operations Manual
5.	Oli	Influencer-at-large
6.	Karen	HR Coordinator
7.	Kassandra?	Accounting Coordinator
8.	Alex?	Influencer-at-large

"Good job," The Catalyst commented. "So, I just want to confirm that these are individuals who can influence how well your new idea is implemented or not. Some confuse Opinion Leaders with stakeholders or groups. Stakeholders are affected by a decision, but they don't necessarily affect it. As we said earlier, groups are influenced by individuals. That's why I'm glad you didn't do that."

Ben nodded, to affirm he understood.

"Tell me about the names and then explain the two with question marks after them."

"Well, as you can see, I included my boss, Sarah, and for the most part, I listed our team leaders we call coordinators, because most of them truly are Opinion Leaders. I wasn't sure about Kassandra. She's a really smart lady, but I'm not sure if she's really an Opinion Leader. She does her job, but I didn't want to leave her out, since I included the other coordinators."

"Do others ask her opinion in meetings?"

"Not really, even though she's smart and a good employee."

"Sounds like I'd take her off the list then," The Catalyst said. "Position and title alone don't qualify for influence."

"Okay, that makes sense. I'll take her off." Ben drew a line through Kassandra's name.

"What about Alex? You included Oli as an influencer-at-large, but not Alex."

"I wasn't sure about him, either. I put Oli on the list because, although he's not a manager, he's been around awhile, and I can tell that others really listen to and respect him. Alex has a lot of the same qualities as Oli, except he's been here less than a year. I can tell he's an up-and-comer."

"If it were me, seems like I'd keep him on the list, because while newness can impact influence, it's more about how you're wired. It's a great opportunity for a new leader to step up. Plus, by elevating him formally or informally, you'll be able tap his power and use him as an ally."

"Good point. I'll keep him on the list."

"Why don't you place a seven beside Alex's name? Anyone else missing?"

Ben wrote a seven on the last line. "I don't think so. I put Sarah on because she obviously has a lot of weight as my supervisor, but I didn't go over her head, because our company gives SVPs a lot of decision-making authority, and I don't think she'd get blocked from anyone over her. Plus, she's delegated authority to me to make whatever changes I deem best."

"From the little Sarah told me about your division, an OL list of seven seems about right. How many employees do you have?"

"We have just over 60."

"As I mentioned before, the rule of thumb is that less than 10% are influencers. The larger the organization, the lower the percent. Twenty or so could represent nearly 1000 employees. It also depends on how authority based or egalitarian your organizational culture is. In large situations, you'd need to strategize how to identify and individually assess those people. If you don't do that, you can easily fail or elevate the pain level of a change project."

"Got it."

"Okay, so hold onto this list. That's the first step in creating the Influence Constellation. The next step is to assess how each of these people is wired when it comes to adopting new ideas. To do that, I need to explain a concept. Years ago, a guy named Everett Rogers wrote an intriguing book called *Diffusion of Innovations*. It's a pithy look at the way new ideas get adopted into society. We don't have time to unpack the whole thing, but he provides a lot of examples of things we do today that reflect how people hold onto traditions, even when they are inefficient and less practical."

"I'll check it out."

"You'll love it. Anyway, one of the things Rogers discusses is the varying rates at which people adopt new ideas. Let me give you a summary. I've changed the labels for these people groups, because some of the terms he used tend to be less flattering. Can I borrow a piece of your paper?"

"Sure." Ben tore a sheet from his notepad and handed it to The Catalyst, who started drawing.

The consultant turned the paper toward Ben. "Okay, here's a typical bell-shaped curve. You see these all the time, illustrating a normal distribution, with most people in the middle and fewer in the two tails." The Catalyst then drew a vertical line about a seventh of the way from the left and wrote a name under the column. "This section represents about 15% and we'll call them Progressives. People on the left end of the curve are the most receptive to innovation and new ideas. They're the ones who stand in lines for the release of breakthrough products. They're the early adopters. They like to be on or near the cutting edge. The 15% includes 2 to 3% of the total who create, the people who come up with breakthrough ideas. The others tend to adopt or innovate them. Society only needs 2 to 3% who create, because it takes so much work to test and develop new ideas and bring them to market."

"That's interesting," Ben said. "I think I'm a Progressive."

"You probably are," The Catalyst responded. "Otherwise, we wouldn't be doing these meetings. The challenge with Creators is that they are not taken seriously by those other than the Progressives, at least not at first. Thus, they don't always have as much influence and power, at least initially. That's why the key is to identify influencers who are non-Creator Progressives, because they possess more influence with the others and embrace new ways of doing things."

"I get it," Ben said.

The Catalyst chuckled. "Someone said that admiration is the feeling you feel, when you meet someone like you."

The men laughed. "So you're saying everyone can't become a Progressive," Ben said.

"That's right, because this has to do with how we're hardwired. These aren't good or bad qualities, in and of themselves. Each category has strengths and weaknesses. It's more about temperament and disposition."

"What's the downside of Progressives?"

"Well, the weakness of Creators, as I said, is they can seem too much like free spirits and flighty, by the large majority. Plus, sometimes they have a difficult time developing a plan. They love a new idea because it's new, not necessarily because it's feasible. Many fall through on follow through, excited by the next new idea."

"What about Progressives?"

"Progressives are less alienated than their Creator cousins, but can get bored quickly and feel impatient with those who aren't as quick to adopt change. Sometimes, they give up on a new idea if it gets too difficult or receives too much pushback. But for the most part, Opinion Leaders who are Progressives are your strongest assets. Creating a change initiative is a bit like making a snowman. The key to a good snowman is starting with a good snowball. You need a tight, hard core so that as you roll it, it holds together and then gathers other snow."

"So, you don't recommend having equal representation from various departments or stakeholder groups?"

"I don't. A lot of people do this, but it's a flawed strategy and part of the reason why so many change projects fail. John Kotter, in his eight-step strategy, refers to this step as building a coalition. New ideas are fragile, like a newborn baby. You want to make sure you protect and gently nurture it. If you invite people who are not wired to accept change or who aren't open to new ideas, their questions and doubts can shut them down."

"I think I get it. That makes me want to rethink who I invite to our early strategy sessions."

"Sometimes, if you can't avoid having certain people in the room, you should create an ad hoc team or skunkworks group, simply to create synergy and early momentum. Remember the law of physics: a body in motion tends to remain in motion, and a body at rest tends to remain at rest. A two-inch block of wood can keep an idle train from moving forward, but the same train going 80 miles per hour can plow through feet of reinforced concrete. New ideas can die easily, so you want to give them a fighting chance."

The Catalyst reached over to the paper and drew a vertical line in the middle of the curve. Then he wrote "Builders" under the column. "The next category of people Rogers identified is what I refer to as the Builders; they make up about 35%. Some refer to them as the early majority. These people are open to workable ideas, but they need to see that it's doable, and it helps if they can see others either using it already or provide a logical plan for it. The challenge with Builders is that sometimes they can get hung up on the details and toss out a new idea, if it's not readily understandable. They say things such as, 'We don't have the money for that' or 'We tried that before' or 'We don't have enough people.' This can end a new idea before it's had time to incubate."

Ben laughed. "Several people came to mind as you were describing this group. We certainly have some Builders in our company."

The Catalyst reached over to the paper and, with his pen, traced the first line several times, making it bolder. Then he drew an arrow at the top of the line and wrote, "chasm." "A guy named Geoffrey Moore wrote a book titled *Crossing the Chasm*. It explains the gap between the Progressives and the rest. If you want an idea, product, or service to become mainstream, you need to cross the chasm between the early adopters and the large majority. Progressives embrace new things more easily and try them; they're willing to take a risk. They stand in line for the new iPhone or latest technology. But you'll never reach critical mass until you pass this tipping point."

"That's interesting," Ben remarked, leaning back and locking his hands behind his head. "I've often wondered why some great products I've discovered never become more popular."

"That may be why." The Catalyst leaned forward and drew another vertical line on the graph, about a seventh of the way from the right end of the curve. Under the third column he wrote the word "Foundationals" and under the fourth, "Anchors." "On the other side of the Builders are the Foundationals, also known as the late majority. This 35% of people wait until they see a large number of people adopting a new product or practice. They tend to take their cues from the Builders. The strength of Foundationals is that they make us think through our ideas. You wouldn't want to fly a plane built solely by Progressives. Foundationals make sure it's safe. Their push back can make things better, much better, even if it frustrates the idea people. The downside is that they can come across as negative. They often have a more difficult time seeing the benefits in a new idea. The Progressive slogan is 'I'll see it when I believe it.' The Foundational slogan is 'I'll believe it when I see it.'"

"So how do we win them over?"

"We as Progressives usually don't. Builders do. Unless you have a close connection with a Foundational or, for some personal reason, a Foundational Opinion Leader values what you're pitching, it's a tough sell for a Progressive leader. Allying with a Builder speeds the process."

"Again, faces come to mind as you describe this group."

"That's good," The Catalyst said. "Leaders need to be thinking this way, so you can appreciate the strengths and challenges of each category and how to leverage their assets."

"So, what about this last group, the Anchors?"

"Well, like their name implies, they provide ballast for an ever-changing society, keeping us moored and appreciative of our heritage. This 15% often gets stereotyped, especially among Progressives. We refer to them as a stick in the mud, ball and chain, old fuddy-duddy, or worse. If you only think of them negatively, they'll often respond in kind. The Pygmalion effect says that people tend to become as they're treated."

"So, what's the downside?"

"Well, just as a strong Anchor Opinion Leader can keep a ship from drifting, he or she can also sink the ship. These people enter the future kicking and screaming. Using the Moses example, many prefer to die in the wilderness than enter the land flowing with milk and honey, for fear of the giants. While they cause tension for Progressive leaders, they actually need a hug more than a flogging. Their negativity and resistance are often symptoms of fear."

"This is all so fascinating," Ben said. "It makes total sense because I can see all of these people in our company. I guess I've been prone to dismiss those who differ from the way I view things."

"We all do. But understanding the rate that various people diffuse innovation helps you bring them along. You're not going to turn a Foundational into a Progressive, but you want to help them see the benefits of your new idea. The goal isn't to have them push the accelerator, but rather take their foot off the brake." The Catalyst paused as Ben made more notes. "Let's take a little pause here, grab a fresh coffee and, when we come back, we'll combine this info for the second step of our Influence Constellation."

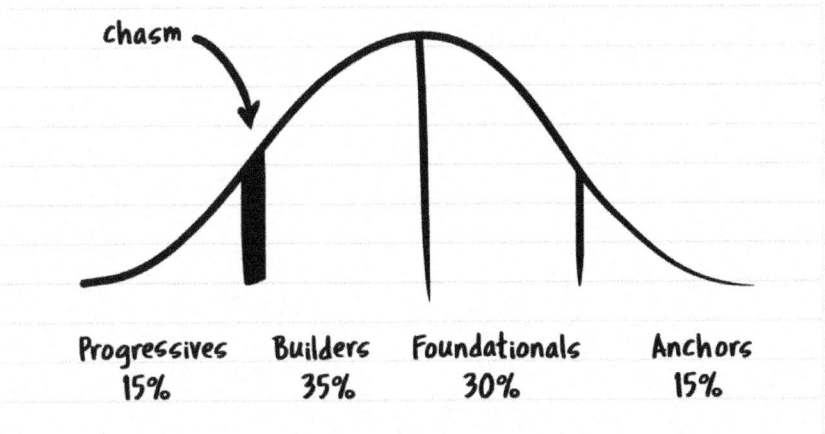

Meeting Notes:
- People in official positions aren't necessarily Opinion Leaders
- People tend to adopt new ideas at varying rates
- Progressives, early adopters (15%), are vital to developing new ideas
- Builders, the early majority (35%), need to see workability; can get stuck on the how
- For ideas to become mainstream, they must cross the chasm between Progressives and Builders
- Foundationals, the late majority (35%), help improve ideas, tend to take cues from Builders
- Anchors, about 15%, often mask their fear with negativity
- Don't expect the right half to push the accelerator; goal is to get their feet off the brake

FIVE STAR CHANGE

chapter five

The two men returned to their table, coffee refills in hand.

"Alright, now that we have something to work with, let's start the first phase of the change model, the Influence Constellation," The Catalyst said.

"What's that?"

"An Influence Constellation is a visual projection of the Opinion Leaders, how they're wired, the size of their influence, whether they are for or against a specific new idea, and the potential influence they have among themselves. It is to a change agent what a blueprint is to a contractor or a battlefield plan is to a military commander. You're going to need a fresh sheet of paper. Then, draw three concentric circles."

Ben ripped out a blank sheet and drew three circles.

"We talked about four types of people in terms of how readily they tend to adopt change. So, in your inner circle write 'Progressives.' We'll assume Creators are part of this group. In the next circle write 'Builders.' In the third circle write 'Foundationals,' and outside the circles write the word 'Anchors.'"

Ben followed The Catalyst's directions. "Now, take your list of people and place each Opinion Leader's corresponding number where you think he or she is in terms of their wiring. Since you dropped Kassandra from your list, just give number seven to Alex. Base this on what you know about them and how they've responded by new ideas in the past."

Ben thoughtfully placed the seven numbers in various circles, then he looked up.

"Do you feel good about that?"

"I do," Ben said.

"Now, give yourself number 8 and place it on the graphic."

Ben wrote an 8 in the Progressives circle.

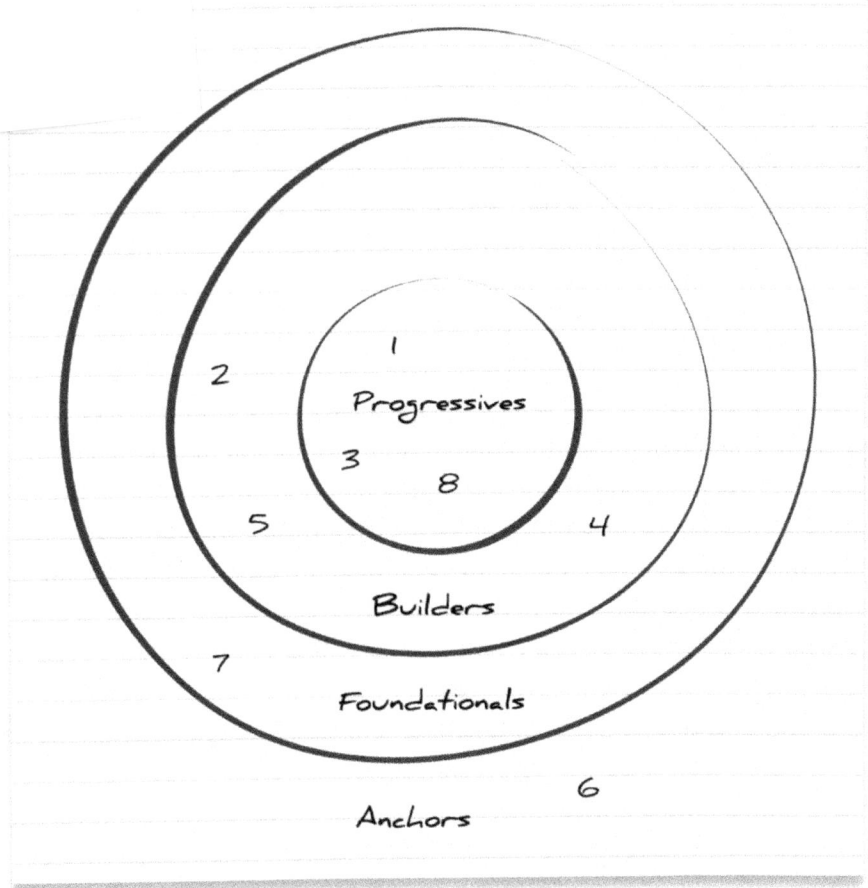

"That's what I assumed," The Catalyst said. "Now we're going to do three more things to this graphic. First, I want you to estimate the size of influence each Opinion Leader has, either small, medium, or large. It may have to do with how many people are in their department or team, or it may simply be how many others turn their heads when they speak. They're all Opinion Leaders, but, naturally, their power and influence will not be the same. Place an 'A' beside the number of those with large influence, a 'B' next to those with medium influence, and a 'C' for those with small influence."

Ben pondered this a few minutes, wrote the letters, and then turned the page to show The Catalyst.

"Good. We could do other analyses, such as looking at the types of influence a person has, whether it's authority, based on position or personality, friendships, or nepotism, like a family member. This helps us see who is connected and how. But, for now, let's do another layer, based on each person's opinion on the specific change you're advocating."

"How is this different than the circles I put them in?" Ben asked.

"It's different because, although our wiring is usually a good predictor of a person's response to change, sometimes an individual will accept or reject an idea based on something else. For example, let's say that you have an Anchor who typically enjoys status quo and bucks progress. But what if you're thinking about starting a new product line that his children would love or, perhaps, opening new employment opportunities for his family members? Although he'd typically push back on such an idea, because he has a vested interest in it, he may embrace it."

"That makes sense."

"What if you don't know where a person stands on a specific issue?"

"You can make an estimated guess or, better yet, have a coffee or lunch with the person, to get feelers on where he or she might stand on it. This info is important for developing an effective Transition Plan. Knowing where all of your OLs stand on a new idea is paramount."

"Okay, how do I denote this?"

"If the Opinion Leader is for the change, put a triangle beside the number. Delta, in the Greek alphabet, has a similar shape and is often used to represent change. Place a circle beside a person who seems neutral, meaning they go round and round without necessarily being for or against it. Put a square beside an OL who is against the idea, because that person wants to block it."

Ben laughed. "Or that you think they're square."

The Catalyst chuckled. "That's true, but we're trying to be descriptive more than judgmental. That could be true, though."

Ben took a few more minutes to place the symbols beside each number and letter, representing his list of Opinion Leaders. He gave it a second look and then turned the page to show The Catalyst.

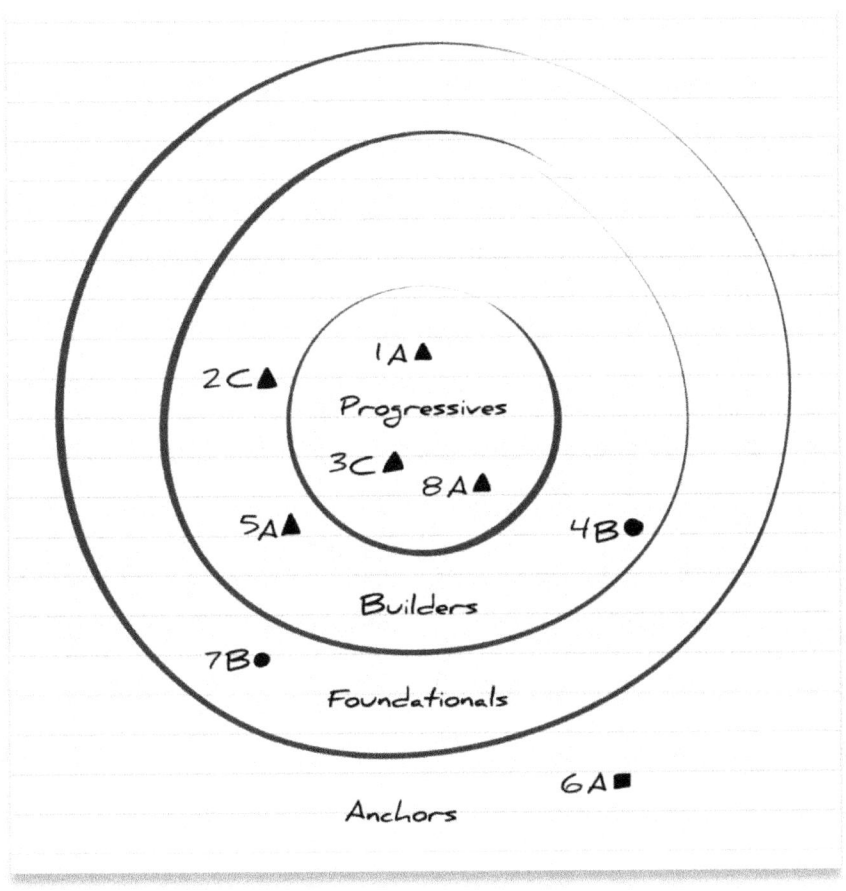

"That's great. Now, one more thing. I want you to add Influence Vectors. Think of who has influence with and over each other as OLs. This may be due to a unique friendship or past interactions. You'll draw an arrow from the person with influence to the other, on the graphic."

Ben looked at the graphic. "Can you give me an example of an Influence Vector?"

"Sure. Let's say that Julie, #3, rated as a 5, in favor of the idea, is a close friend with Alex, #6, who is a 2. If her influence is stronger than yours as the leader, Julie could help sway him. At the same time, if Alex has more influence with Julie than you do, he could dissuade her support of the innovation, weakening her excitement, moving her from a 5 to a 4."

"Oh, that's interesting. This feels like a game of chess."

"Chess or three-dimensional tug of war, you get it," The Catalyst said. "Power and influence are strategic. Those who succeed know how to read social dynamics and use them to their advantage."

"Isn't that manipulation?"

"If you use it selfishly, it is. But, if you use if for mutual good and to benefit the organization, it's persuasion. Intent changes the character of an action."

Ben worked in silence for a few minutes and then turned the paper toward The Catalyst, who gave it a lingering look and then said, "Good job. You ready for what's next?"

"I can't wait," Ben said, smiling.

FIVE STAR CHANGE

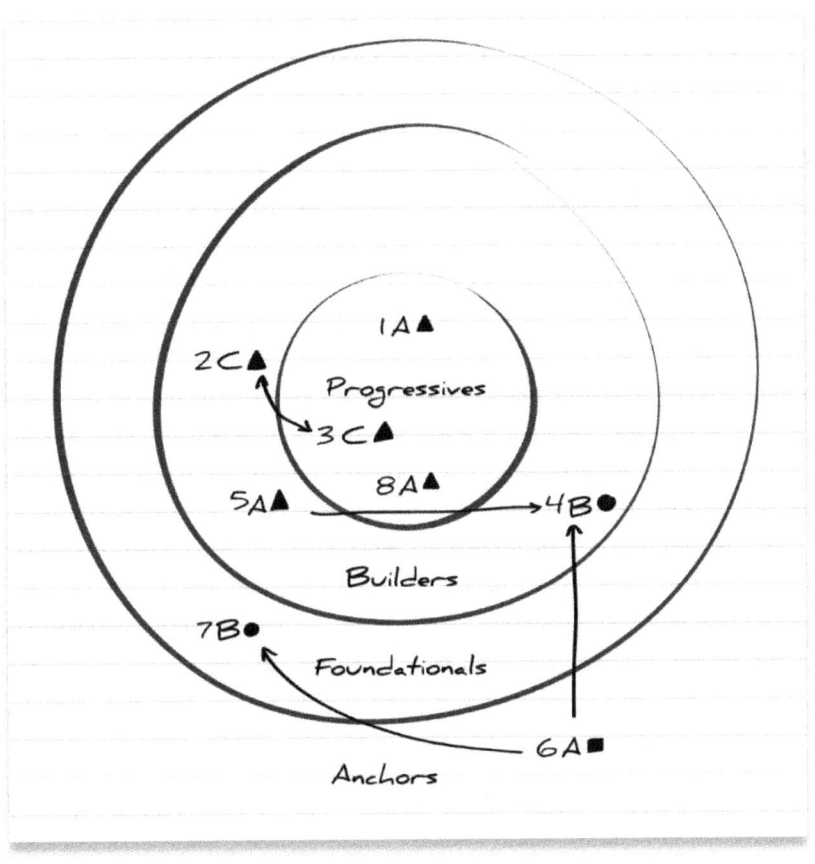

Meeting Notes:
- The Influence Constellation is the 1st of 3 NCM components. It's a visual projection of the Opinion Leaders (OL), how they're wired, the size of their influence, whether they are for or against a specific idea, and influence they have among themselves.
- Consider if the OLs are Progressives, Builders, Foundationals, or Anchors
- Consider the size of influence an OL has in the organization (A = lg., B = med., C = small).
- Consider if the OL is for (,), neutral (,) or against ( ) the specific idea. An OL's opinion of a specific idea may not parallel his/her normal wiring.
- Influence Vectors depict power among OLs, noting who could influence another, both positively or negatively.

chapter six

"All right, the Influence Constellation you just did is the first phase of the NCM. The next is a four-factor formula that gives us important info for designing a Five-Star Change transition plan," The Catalyst explained. "So, turn back to your list of the Opinion Leaders."

Ben turned to the page in his notepad.

"As you look at the list, you want to estimate how each Opinion Leader will respond to the proposed change, on a scale of one to five."

"A Likert Scale."

"Right. Since you know what a Likert scale is, you might find this bit of background interesting. Rensis Likert created this tool in 1932 for measuring opinion. It's the basis of the typical social survey. He also introduced the concept of participative management, so in this sense, we're using them together."

"How interesting," Ben said.

"Originally the Likert scale involved seven scores, but we'll be using five. In this case, a score of 1 is if the OL opposes and may try to block the idea. A 2 is if the person dislikes, but won't fight it. A value of 3 represents a neutral opinion, neither for nor against. A 4 is if a person favors, and a 5 is if someone approves of and will likely help sell the idea to others."

"So, you want me to write a numerical estimate for each person on the list?"

"Yes. Each score is called a Likert item. You'll do one for everyone except you. You're the leader, so we'll talk about that factor next."

Ben looked at the list and began writing a number beside each person. He spent more time thinking about a couple names. Then he turned the paper to show The Catalyst.

1. Sarah	SVP
2. John	Marketing Coordinator
3. Julie	Sales Coordinator
4. Michael	Operations Manual
5. Oli	Influencer-at-large
6. Karen	HR Coordinator
~~7. Kassandra?~~	~~Accounting Coordinator~~
7. ~~8.~~ Alex?	Influencer-at-large

"Okay, good. I'm glad you included your boss Sarah among your Opinion Leaders. I wanted to see what score you'd give her. In this case, you should do that. At the same time, I get a sense that she's expecting you to do this change project on your own. Am I right?"

"Pretty much," Ben answered. "She said that she'll support my idea, but wanted me to run with it."

"Okay, so you're going to figure the average for your Opinion Leaders, but let's keep her score out of it, because you're primarily interested on the OLs in your division. You'll keep her support as a safety net, sort of in your back pocket, but both she and you want the change to come from within your own team."

"That makes sense."

"The NCM provides structure, but it's also flexible. Every situation is different, so you need to deal with the anomalies that make them unique. This is what critical thinking is about. So, average the scores for the people you listed, except for Sarah."

Ben added the total of the six estimates in his head and then divided by six. "It's 3.5."

"So, it's halfway between neutral and favorable, based on the one to five scale. This number is called the Influencer Readiness. It's a numerical estimate of how ready your Opinion Leaders are to adopt the new idea. We'll come back to that figure in a few minutes, when we tabulate the formula. In fact, let me show you where we're going with this. Can I borrow another sheet of your paper?"

"Sure." Ben tore out a sheet and slid it to The Catalyst, who took out his pen and wrote on it. He then turned the sheet around and showed it to Ben.

$$\frac{(LC + IR) \times T}{II} = TI$$

"Here's the mathematical formula, based on four factors that will give us a result called the Transition Index. I'll explain what each means as we come to it. We just determined the IR, which stands for Influencer Readiness. It's 3.5. So, go ahead and write 3.5 beside the IR on the formula. Let's look at the other three factors now. Let's do the LC. That stands for Leader Capacity," The Catalyst explained, pointing to it on the paper.

"What's that?"

"Leader Capacity is the ability to lead that the person in charge has, not just be the boss. In this case, you're the leader. Leaders by nature are change agents. Managers are not. Leaders like to charge the gates. Managers prefer to hold the fort. A strong leader is good at selling a vision, developing trust, and building a coalition. A weak leader is not."

"Uh oh, I see where this is heading," Ben said with a nervous smile. "Am I going to have to estimate my own Leader Capacity?"

The Catalyst chuckled. "You're getting ahead of me a bit, but yes, you will."

"What's the deal about leading versus managing? Why do you distinguish between the two?"

"Fair question, since most people use leader, boss, manager, and supervisor synonymously. At the end of the day, most bosses and supervisors need to be able to do both at times. Whether or not they do them well is a different matter. Most do not, as they are unique from each other. Leaders tend to lean into change. Managers can do this, but on a much smaller scale, making incremental improvements. Leaders tend to be stronger on the people side, whereas managers focus more on task and process.

"Zaleznik, a former Harvard professor, introduced these ideas decades ago. Kotter said that managers make sure things are done right, whereas leaders strive to introduce the right things we should be doing. There is a mindset difference between the two, and it tends to muddy the understanding when people don't distinguish between them."

Ben looked up from his notes. "I get this. It makes so much sense. I think of the bosses I've had over the years and it really explains a lot."

"I'm not trying to say that managing is bad and leading is good," The Catalyst explained. "You almost always need managing, to keep the systems running and maintaining operations. That's no easy task. But when change is needed, managing falls short. It won't do what needs to be done."

"It's like great pitching versus great hitting," Ben said. "You need both, but great pitchers are rarely good behind the plate."

"I like that," The Catalyst affirmed. "You need strong defense and offense, but they are different animals."

"Okay, so what's the 1 to 5 scale for Leader Capacity?"

"Well, 1 means very little observable capacity. There may be intelligence and talent, but not so much in the area of leading. The boss may be well liked, but not necessarily respected for his or her ability to lead. A 2 means that the leader is low in leadership. A 3 means some leadership capacity is evident. A 4 is strong, and a 5 is very strong."

"What if a leader is new in a supervisory role? Won't the number go up over time?"

"Well, yes and no. A person's Leader Capacity will go up if he or she leads well, gains allegiance, and proves him or herself. Usually, we offer a new supervisor influence credit, based on a good reputation and resume. But if a person doesn't exemplify strong leadership, people skills, and decision making, he or she will go down in influence. A powerless leader is an oxymoron, because you can't lead without power."

"That's interesting. I love this stuff," Ben said.

The Catalyst chuckled. "Most leaders do. But let me give you an exception to this rule, in the context of the formula. If you're in an authority-based organization, such as the military, paramilitary, or a government agency, where the person holding the highest position makes the decision regardless of his or her ability to lead, then you don't estimate the capacity, but rather simply that person's opinion."

"Run that by me again."

"Basically, in authority-oriented organizations, where power is primarily positional more than it is the individual's ability to lead, then the score you give to the Leader Capacity goes back to that person's view of the innovation, just like in the Opinion Leaders. For example, a leader who is a 1, meaning they're against the idea, can pretty much block the change from happening, based on rank. But if you're a captain in the army, against a proposed change, yet your general is a 5, meaning he or she is highly in favor of it, chances are slim you'll get your way. Therefore, the opinion of the highest-ranking individual is what we use for the LC factor in authority-based organizations."

"So, doesn't a person's title or position always factor into the formula?"

"It's a factor, but in most organizations, say 80% or so, it's more about the individual supervisor's ability to lead that will determine the outcome. The leader is the person primarily in

charge of the decision, most responsible for making the change happen or not."

"So, in my case, it's me, even though I have a boss?" Ben asked.

"In this situation, it sounds like it, since your boss is pretty much giving you the authority to call the shot. That's delegation. But you still have to work with your team and your various managers. Thus, it comes down to your ability to sell them on the change and organize it in such a way that you'll get buy-in from the others. It's the difference between compliance and commitment."

"How so?"

"What most civilians don't understand about the military is they think that just because a person with a high rank says something, everyone does it. That's compliance. But what you want even more in battle is commitment, people who don't just obey commands but are willing to sacrifice and stay engaged. In today's world and in most business situations, compliance won't cut it. People have too many other options. They'll either quit, go find another job, or worse, they'll stay in your company, under perform, and secretly sabotage the new idea. Passive-aggressive behaviors are pervasive in businesses. So, once again, it comes down to leadership for implementing change that isn't a slam dunk."

Ben pondered The Catalyst's comments. "That's so interesting. So, I need to estimate my Leader Capacity."

"You do."

"Okay, then if I'm honest with you, I'd rate my LC as a 4. I feel like I've proven myself and have good rapport with my team, but I haven't been in this role a long time. I am comfortable making difficult decisions. I think most of my people trust me and would go with me. But for a change this large, it would be better if I had another year or two of wins under my belt."

"Okay, good explanation, so 4 it is. Go ahead and write a 4 beside LC on the diagram. Then, we'll get to the third factor in the formula," The Catalyst said. "It's usually the most pivotal one."

Meeting Notes:
- The 2nd component of NCM is a 4-factor formula resulting in a numerical estimate to predict the efficacy of a change transition
- One factor is Influence Readiness (IR), an average of all of the individual OL estimates on a 1-to-5 scale, with 1 being strongly against and 5 strongly in favor
- A 2nd factor is Leader Capacity (LC), an estimate of the person in charge's ability to lead on a 1-to-5 scale, 1 being very low and 5 very high
- In authority-based organizations, such as the military or government, the LC can reflect the highest-ranking person's opinion on the idea

chapter seven

"Now, it's time to talk about . . . Time, represented by the T in the formula. Time is often the most flexible of the four factors. A lot of leaders never reach Five-Star Change because they try to push change too fast. Leaders are notorious for picking a deadline out of thin air and then basing everything on that date."

"That's interesting. We may have done that a bit, when I think about it."

"The ancient Greeks had two words for time. One was *chronos*, where we get the word chronology. This focuses on a quantity of time. In Western society, it's primarily how we think of time. The meeting will last two hours. We begin at 9am. Profits will be such and such at the end of the quarter. But the other Greek word for time was *kairos*. It's about quality of time. This is more of an Eastern concept. I grew up on a farm in Iowa and, every fall, my dad and I started walking into the corn fields. He'd take an ear from the stalk, pull down the husks, and press his thumbnail into the kernels. We'd do this a couple times a week. Then one day, my dad would say, 'It's time to pick the corn.' Even though the seed hybrid might say 80 days from planting to harvesting, farmers knew this varied, based on the heat, rainfall, and soil type. So even though Time in our change model is based on *chronos*, quantity, transitioning is more about *kairos*, quality. A Transition Index focuses on readiness for a change, much like a farmer looks at a crop's maturation for harvest. That's the goal of this formula and ultimately your Transition Plan."

"So how do you select a time?"

"Sometimes you have a hard deadline, such as a pending merger, or a patent ending, or a balloon payment on a loan, but more often it's an artificial and highly subjective decision."

"I think we sort of took a guestimate of how long we thought it should take, but we didn't have a hard timeline to follow," Ben admitted.

"That's good to know, because after we use the formula, it may be something we can adjust. Let's revisit this after we do the math, because your current time may be fine. My point is that, usually, this is the most flexible of the four factors in case we see the Transition Index denotes a potential problem. If it's inflexible, then we'll need to focus on the other factors."

"Why do you multiply the Time factor in the formula, but you add Leader Capacity and Influencer Readiness?"

"Good question. You add Leader Capacity and Influencer Readiness, because they represent the people components, the psychological aspect. Time is a multiplier, because it takes time for people to adopt a new idea. The faster you go, the more difficult it is and more likely they'll rebel."

Ben pondered the explanation. "Okay, so do you use a 1 to 5 scale for Time?"

"We do. Here are the five values. A level 1 is fast, less than six months. This is like a microwave oven, because for a significant innovation, it's quick."

"So why is less time a low number and longer time a high one?"

"Because, in the mathematical formula it's a dividend. It's on the top, so the faster you go, the smaller the top number will be, decreasing the Transition Index and probably making Five-Star Change less of a possibility. You'll see how it impacts it when we have all of the numbers, but speed can kill when it comes to driving on the road and driving change in an organization."

"Okay."

"A 2 represents six up to twelve months. A 3 is between one and two years. This is the equivalent of a conventional oven. A 4 is three to four years and a 5 value is five years, more like a crockpot."

Ben wrote these in his notes. "Why did you stop at five years? What about a 10- or 20-year plan?"

"The reason is that, at the rapid rate of change these days, futurists say it's very difficult to adequately plan more than five years in advance. It doesn't mean you shouldn't, but the time we're talking about here is the time between launching a specific change to fully implementing it."

"Ah, that makes sense."

"There's some wiggle room in terms of brainstorming and planning, but it has to do with how long people have to embrace it and accept it. So, based on these numbers, what estimate would you give to your Time factor?"

"Well, our goal was six to twelve months, so that would be a 2, but now that you mention it, maybe we could do it at a slower pace."

"Okay," The Catalyst said. "Go ahead and write a 2 on the formula, but if extending Time is an option, we may revisit it if needed." Ben put a 2 beside the T on the formula. "Good, now let's analyze the fourth factor. The II stands for Idea Impact. This has to do with the size of the innovation. Naturally, the larger the change, the more difficult it will be to embrace it. That's why we place this estimate as the divisor. A trip from LA to New York takes a lot more effort than driving to Santa Barbara, but a lot less effort than going to China."

"What are the numerical equivalents?"

"So, using the same 1 to 5 scale, a 1 represents a very small impact. Let me use cardio health as a metaphor. It's like when the doctor says you need to eat better and exercise. That's a 1 on our scale. A level 2 impact represents larger change; it's still minor overall. In our metaphor, it's equivalent to a doctor prescribing a med to lower your blood pressure or reduce your cholesterol. A level 3 Idea Impact is substantial. This change will be felt by everyone in the organization where it's adopted. In our metaphor, it's similar to angioplasty. A level 4 impact is very significant. It's similar to bypass surgery. It's a big deal. A change of this size will significantly disrupt the way you do business, at least for a while."

"If that's a 4, then what's a 5?" Ben asked.

"A 5 is transformational. It's equivalent to a heart transplant. In terms of organizational impact, people who knew the company before the change may not recognize it after. It will transform the way you operate and may even alter your mission and philosophy."

"Hmm, that's interesting. So, what's the strategy in getting this factor correct?"

"The rule of thumb is to begin at 3 and then raise or lower it, based on the description I gave. People tend to overestimate the impact. They say it's a 4 or 5 when it's not. If it changes how you do things, as opposed to what your final outcome is, then it's probably not a 4 or 5. Things such as software programs, new policies and protocols, are usually in the 1 to 2 range, even if they're uncomfortable for a while. An overhaul of the culture or a significant restructure is probably more of a 3 or 4. A change in mission, such as moving from brick and mortar to operating virtually, may be a 5."

"So, if you're going through a change process, is it smarter to make a lot of changes all at once?"

"Interesting question. That's another mistake many leaders make, thinking they should make all the changes at one time. While there may be wisdom with that, remember that change creates stress, so it's usually smart to begin with changes that yield the most results, so people can see benefits from their efforts. Imagine if every Saturday night, when your local grocery store closed, they decided to reorganize everything and change the aisles. The next day you walk in, the bakery is on the left instead of the right, and the milk is on aisle three instead of in the back. After a couple of weeks, everyone would stop shopping at that store, because it would drive them crazy.

"Change creates stress, so if you add too much at a time, it can overwhelm people, and they shut down emotionally and cognitively. The key is to do what will produce the best results, not try to do everything at once. You may decide to roll out small changes first, to develop trust and build on the wins. But if this takes too long, more substantial changes may be required. Trying to swallow too much food at once can choke a person. Swallowing too much change can choke an organization."

"That makes a lot of sense," Ben said. "So, I think the Idea Impact we're considering is a 4 because it's a pretty big deal for us. This is a major restructure, not a minor one. There may be some things we could do to reduce it to a 3, but we'd need to ponder this more."

"I like the way you're thinking," The Catalyst affirmed. "Considering options is valuable as you do the math and determine whether you need to make room to modify the results. So, for now, why don't you put a 4 beside the II in the formula and then we'll do the calcs."

Ben wrote a 4 in the formula.

The Catalyst looked at his watch. "Hey, it's close to lunch time. How about if we go to Mediterraneo, an Italian restaurant just up the sidewalk, where we can discuss the Transition Index?"

"Oh, noooo! Don't leave me hanging."

"Delay of gratification, my friend. Good things come to those who wait. The change of venue will be good for us, pun intended. Their chairs are softer, too," The Catalyst said, smiling.

Ben was excited and a bit anxious to see what the NCM would infer about the change project.

Meeting Notes:
- A 3rd factor in the NCM formula is Time, often the most flexible of the four.
- Time generally refers to when an idea is formally announced to when it's fully implemented.
- Western society thinks in terms of time quantity (chronos). Other parts of the world think of time quality (kairos); transition plans emphasize the latter.
- Time is a multiplier because the less the time, generally the greater the stress.
- NCM Time values: 0-<6 mo. = 1, 6-<12 mo. = 2, 1-2 yrs. = 3, 3-4 yrs = 5, 5 yrs. = 5
- Transitions over 5 yrs. are difficult to plan because of the rate of change in society.
- A 4th factor in the NCM formula is Idea Impact, how much the innovation will change status quo of an organization, on a 1-to-5 scale (1 low, 5 high)
- The tendency is to over-estimate Idea Impact; 1 is minor, 5 is very large and rare; i.e. mission change; transformation; people who knew the org before the change may not recognize it after

chapter eight

Once inside the restaurant, the two men were ushered to the patio, overlooking a lagoon with a fountain.

"Nice setting, isn't it?" The Catalyst suggested.

"Gorgeous," Ben answered. "You pick some great venues to meet."

"I want to convey the sense of Five-Star quality," The Catalyst said with a smile.

As soon as the men ordered lunch, Ben pulled out the NCM formula worksheet. "Okay, I'm chomping at the bit to run the numbers and see how it looks to you."

The Catalyst chuckled. "All right, run the math on the numbers you entered."

Ben pulled out his phone and opened the calculator app, mumbling the numbers to himself as he entered them. "Okay, it comes out to be 3.75."

"All right. That's your Transition Index, so write that beside the TI on the sheet."

$$\frac{(LC^4 + IR^{3.5}) \times T^2}{II^4} = TI\ 3.75$$

"So, is it good, bad, or what?"

"Can you hand me another sheet of paper? Let's see where your Transition Index falls on a graphic."

Ben pulled out a clean sheet and slid it to The Catalyst, who began drawing. After a minute, he turned the page toward Ben.

"This represents the third component of the NCM. It's the Transition Index Analysis. We're going to estimate transition efficacy, based on the formula calculations, and then strategize how we can improve the outcome.

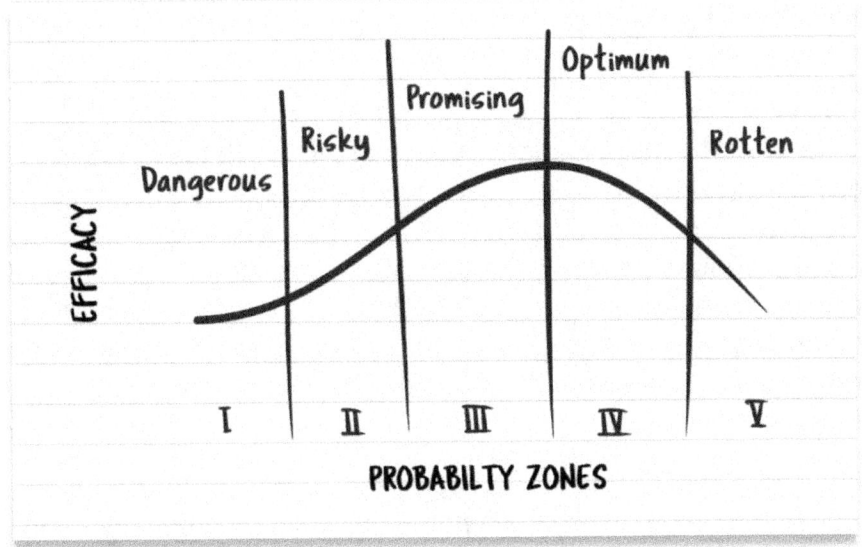

"There are five categories called Probability Zones. I call them that because they predict the probability of seeing Five-Star Change happen, which is the highest level of efficacy." The Catalyst pointed to the left side of the graph with the word "Dangerous" on it and wrote the numbers "0.4-1.5." He continued, "As you can see by the descriptor of Zone One, this is not a good place to be. It's dangerous. Fat chance the change will happen. A Transition Index at this level would result in significant pain for the organization. People are likely to quit and the shock of the transition might be overwhelming. The patient might die on the operating table, even if it's the correct diagnosis. Most of the time, changes at this level are rejected. They're among the 70% that Kotter said don't happen. Promoting change in Zone One would be irresponsible and only recommended as a last-ditch effort."

The Catalyst leaned forward and wrote "1.6-2.9" in the second column on the graph. "Zone Two is a Transition Index range of 1.6 to 2.9. It's 'Risky,' meaning if you're betting on a horse race, your horse is a long shot. Again, more than likely, a change project will be rejected here. It's among the 70% that fail."

"So, I'm sure this is a naïve question, but what's wrong with rolling the dice?"

"If the idea is important, why would you roll the dice? Why leave it to luck? The only time you'd want to move forward in this zone is if it's a trivial matter or you're in a crisis. If the risk of not doing it exceeds the risk of doing it, you may need to move forward, but don't be surprised if it fails. It was predictable. Another reason not to roll the dice is that, the more times people experience a flawed change effort, the more difficult it is for them to adopt one in the future. Don't make me quote the Mark Twain 'cat on a hot stove' statement again," The Catalyst said with a smile.

"One of the reasons people resist change efforts so much is that, over the course of a lifetime, most have experienced any number of terrible transitions, inoculating them to organizational changes in general, even those necessary for improvement or to thwart decay."

"Makes sense. Please, go on."

The Catalyst wrote "3-7.9" in the third column. "Zone Three is called 'Promising.' It's for Transition Indices between 3 and 7.9. A TI in this zone shows possibilities. I used to call it 'positive,' but soon learned that people felt good if their score landed here, so they did little to improve it. Scores within this zone can be deceiving, because we may feel good about them and think it won't be that difficult. The problem is that it will still produce pain and, if we missed something, we'll be in big trouble. There's very little margin for error here, and Five-Star Change rarely happens in this zone. You'll have to settle for a lower quality transition, when often it's unnecessary."

"So, our current score came out to be 3.75, meaning it's in the lower end of this zone."

"That's right, so naturally, you have some good things going for you, but we'll want to take a closer look and try to figure out how we can move it toward the 'Optimum' range. Let me explain the last two zones and then we'll come back to your TI."

"Got it."

"Zone Four is Optimum, for Transition Indices in the 8-20 range," The Catalyst said, as he wrote in the numbers. "This means there's a good chance your transition will go well."

"So obviously my Transition Index isn't there yet," said Ben, "but if you run your numbers through the NCM and land in Zone Four, isn't that a slam dunk?"

"Slam dunks are rare in organizational change. You still need to finish your homework and due diligence. As long as it's the right idea, it will likely happen and create strong results. Optimum Transition Index scores don't mean they're a slam dunk, but rather the chance of Five-Star Change is most likely. One thing I'd do, if I landed in this zone, is run a premortem at the start."

"A what?"

"A premortem. Chances are you've heard of a postmortem," The Catalyst said.

"Sure, that's like doing an autopsy on a project, figuring out what went well and what didn't."

"Correct. It's also known as an AAR, after action report, focusing on how to improve the next time. A premortem is what you do before you execute a plan. A guy named Gary Klein came up with the concept. You start by assuming the plan fails and then you brainstorm reasons why it failed. Sometimes, you uncover things you overlooked."

"Interesting," Ben said, writing notes.

The Catalyst then pointed to the right side of the graph. "The fifth zone is titled 'Rotten,' for scores 21 through 50."

"Up to now, higher Transition Index scores are good, so why isn't this the best?" Ben asked.

"The problem with Zone Five is that, most of the time, if you've waited until this point to implement the new idea, you've lost potential. It's like waiting for all the fruit to be ready before you start picking. If you do that, some will have rotted. When leaders wait until everyone is on board, chances are they've lost the trust of their Progressives, who either quit, transfer, or simply lose faith in management's ability. Effective leaders don't let this happen. Managers often do. Either way, you've decreased momentum or let the competition get a jump on you. It's not a good place to be."

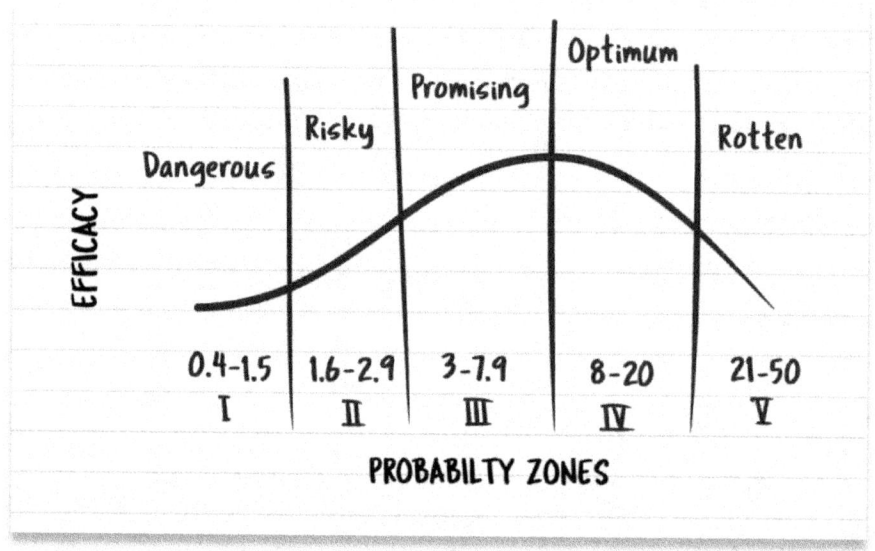

Ben wrote more notes. Then he looked up and asked, "So what do I need to do about our 3.75 Transition Index?"

"Let me turn that back to you. Knowing the formula and doing the math, what do you think you can do?"

Ben bit his lip as he thought. Then he said, "Well, I already mentioned that I could probably extend the Time a bit, since it was a somewhat subjective deadline. Adding a few months wouldn't hinder the idea and it would move the T factor from a 2 to a 3."

"That's good, so long as you're actually doing something in the added time to ready your people, not just extending the schedule."

"Got it. I may also rethink the Idea Impact, per chance that I'm trying to do too much. I'll review that."

"Good. What else?" The Catalyst asked, leaning forward.

Ben thought for a while. "I could work on improving the Influence Readiness average by selling the idea better to some of the lower-rated Opinion Leaders. I'd set up meetings to find out why those who didn't have buy-in didn't like the idea. This might help me know how to sell it better, whether it was education or reframing, perhaps letting them participate more in the planning, so long as they didn't squash the idea."

"Great. Those seem like viable ideas."

"Is there anything I can do to increase Leader Capacity?"

"That's usually the most difficult factor to improve, because personal and professional growth take time. If the leader is on his or her way out, then perhaps you can hope for a stronger leader. Conversely, if you have a strong leader in place, you may want to shorten the time if the leader has announced retirement or, as in the military, a move is likely every three years."

"Wow, that's a lot to think about," Ben added, "but it really makes sense."

"The strong benefit of NCM is that it creates talking points to think critically about key factors in a Transition Plan. So between now and the next time we meet, I want you to come up with a plan of how you can move the TI score to the Optimum Zone, the OZ. I guess that would make you the Wizard of OZ." The Catalyst chuckled. "I never thought of it that way. It's kind of a fun play on words. Okay, any questions?"

"No, it's a lot of info to process, but I feel like I've learned so much. I have a lot to think about."

Ben packed up his notes and the two men walked to the parking lot. As he unlocked his car remotely, it gave a little beep.

"Hey, nice car," The Catalyst commented.

"Thanks," Ben responded. "We just got it. It's so fun."

"I assume it has the indicators that let you know when someone is in your blind spot."

"Those are lifesavers in LA."

"Exactly. Think of the NCM change model you're learning as a radar system to warn you of things in your blind spot. It's unfortunate when leaders get blindsided in transition processes, running into barriers they didn't see. That's the main reason why there's so little Five-Star Change out there. It's not a lack of fortitude or IQ, simply ignorance, a lack of understanding about the transition process."

The men waved goodbye as Ben drove out of the parking lot, down the street, and back onto the 101 toward Los Angeles. His mind swirled with thoughts about what he'd learned from The Catalyst. He began pondering other ways he could improve the Transition Index and make the planned change more effective. He anticipated the next meeting with The Catalyst, even though he sensed that their times together may be nearing an end.

Meeting Notes:
- The 3rd component of NCM is a Transition Index Analysis, noting which of 5 zones it lies in and how to move it to an Optimum range.
- A common temptation is to become complacent with Transition Index scores in the Promising Zone, instead of improving them.
- An Optimum Zone rating doesn't guarantee Five-Star Change, but reflects a strong probability so long as due diligence is fulfilled.
- A premortem is process that assumes a plan fails before it's executed, to brainstorm potentially overlooked challenges.
- The primary purpose of NCM is to reduce the size of org change blind spots.

chapter nine

"Technology is great, isn't it?" The Catalyst commented, adjusting his webcam.

"It is," Ben responded. "Thanks so much for pivoting for my sake. I got called out of town for a big meeting."

"No worries. I'm glad we're able to continue our conversation. I don't know how much more I can teach you, but progress is good."

Ben chuckled. "I doubt I've begun to learn all I can from you, but I so appreciate your investment."

"So how is the Transition Index modification coming?"

"Well, I looked over the Idea Impact and feel like we can reduce it to a 3, if we brainstorm ways of keeping more of our staff in the restructure. Plus, I removed a few items that were more cosmetic than anything. As we discussed, I've decided to extend the time another six to twelve months, moving that from a 2 to a 3. We'll develop customized strategies for Karen, to whom I gave a 2 on the Opinion Leaders list. Plus, we've brainstormed strategies for reaching out to Alex and Michael, who are currently at a level 3. The goal is to raise those three OLs by 1 point each. This would give us a Transition Index of 8, on the low end but within the Optimum Zone 4, and thus increase the likelihood of Five-Star Change. I'm currently brainstorming the details with my Progressive coalition team."

"That's great. Sounds like you're processing it well."

"Any more ideas on moving up our lower-rated Opinion Leaders?" Ben asked.

"Sure. First, don't sell the solution. Sell the problem."

"What?"

"I know it's counterintuitive. William Bridges said that, 90% of the time, leaders try to sell their solutions when they should be selling problems. The reason is that adults aren't shopping for a solution for which they don't perceive a problem. People are pragmatic. Whether with data, an outside consultant, comparison with a competitor, or other sort of analysis, you must elevate the need. Someone said, 'You can lead a horse to water, but you can't make him drink. But you can give the horse salt tablets.' In other words, create a thirst or hunger for what you're advocating, before you focus on a way to resolve it."

Ben jotted down the ideas in his notes. "That's good," he said. "Let's say we do this and still can't get the Opinion Leaders to budge? Any other ideas in your toolbox?"

"Actually, there are. I assume you shop at Costco."

"Who doesn't?"

"Ever go around lunch time?"

"You mean for the sample buffet?"

The two men laughed. "Exactly," The Catalyst affirmed. "The power of a sample is it lets us taste before we buy. Plus, there's a thing called the law of reciprocity, meaning we're more likely to feel obliged to buy when we've been given something first."

"Okay, so I take the resistant people to Costco for samples?"

The Catalyst chuckled. "Well, sort of. Actually, if you come to an impasse, consider offering to run the new idea as a pilot, as on a trial basis, for 30, 60, or 90 days, some period of time that makes sense. Another option may be to run it through one part of the division. It has to make sense in the context. By doing this, you're removing the element of the unknown. They get to taste before they buy. Plus, if you do this after they've pushed back, as sort of a concession, it makes it more difficult for them to oppose it, because you've offered an alternative. Chances are they'll reciprocate."

"That's interesting," Ben said. "I like that as a backup strategy."

"Pilot programs can be powerful. If it's a good idea, people realize it's sensible and they get to taste before buying."

"I'm sure I'll have more questions as we activate the Transition Plan, but all of this makes such great sense."

"Good," The Catalyst responded. "Hey, as I was thinking about our meeting today, I thought it might be good to talk about another issue in the transition process that people and organizations typically experience while transitioning. Have you heard of the s-curve?"

"I have. It's about the growth path of a new product or company, right?"

"That's true." The Catalyst began writing on a notepad on his desk. "Hold on a second. I've got a visual for you." He drew on a page and then held up the paper to the camera.

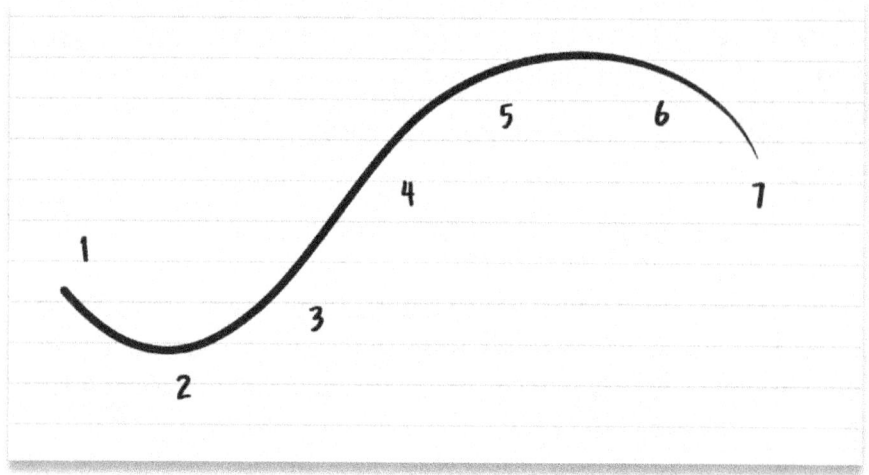

"Every person and every organization have a lifespan. None of us live forever, as we know. I read a while ago that the average duration of an organization in 1950 was about 60 years, but it's now down to around 20. The lifecycle is getting shorter and shorter, meaning this curve is getting steeper and steeper. Thus, survival requires the ability to adapt to an increasingly changing environment.

"Let me explain the stages of the s-curve, as they relate to the evolution of adopting a change. Point 1 represents the inception of a new idea, whether it's an innovation, start-up company, or even conceiving a baby. This is the point of excitement and anticipation. Point 2 is what we call The Dip. It's the time we start wondering what in the world we were thinking when we came up with the idea. This is when you project that 500 people will show up to your restaurant the first week, but only 50 do. It's the 2am feeding of your newborn."

Ben laughed. "I get that."

"This is what Seth Godin talks about in his book, *The Dip*. It's the line between those who persevere and those who quit. Nearly every great endeavor goes through a time like this. It's hitting the wall if you're running a marathon. It's pulling an all-nighter, wrestling over pulling the plug on your start-up or seeing it through. The bottom line is that people who succeed, those who experience greatness, traverse this trough. That's not to say that you should never quit, because sometimes this is when you discover an idea isn't worth the effort. Escalation of commitment is a perception bias that makes us think throwing good money after bad will fix a lousy decision. But if you always quit in the dip, you'll never sip success."

"Sounds like New Year's resolutions," Ben said.

The Catalyst laughed. "It's why you can always find lots of new or slightly used exercise equipment online, three to six months after January."

"Ouch, that one hurt. So, what does this have to do with Five-Star Change?" Ben asked.

"Here, wait a second." The Catalyst started writing again on his notepad. Then, he held up a new page in front of the camera.

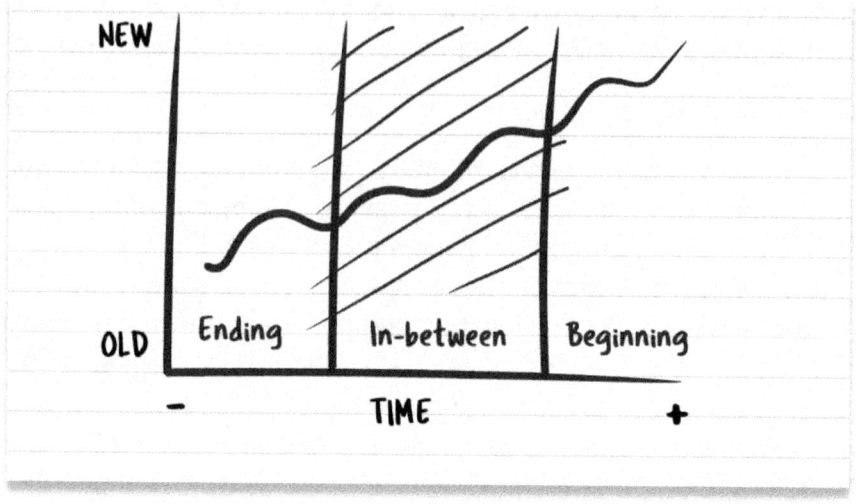

"Imagine this graphic is a close-up of the dip, if you zoomed in. When you're going through a big change, it's not a linear path. It's more like a roller coaster, where at times you feel like you're in a free fall. When you're in an organization, you have people going in and out of three phases, an ending phase, on the left, a beginning phase, on the right, and the in-between phase. Those in the ending phase are grieving what is lost, what they'll miss, the good ol' days. Employees in the beginning phase are celebrating change, what is new and hopeful. The in-between phase is when you feel out of control. It's the anxiety of the trapeze artist who has let go of one bar, but not yet grabbed the next."

"What does this mean for me as a leader? How do I know who is in what phase and how to help them?"

"Love the way you're thinking," The Catalyst said. "The funny thing is, at any given time, your people may be in any of these phases. As you see by the upward weaving line in the graphic, it's not a straight path. It's often more like a zigzag. On one day, a person may be mourning the ending of old things. The next day she is in the turmoil phase, between ending and beginning. The day after, she's back to focusing on the losses. But in a week, the same person could claim how excited she is about the changes. So, while time helps people adopt new things, they do so at varying rates and not always sequentially, meaning it can vacillate from day to day, week to week. You may have a staff meeting with attendees in each phase. At that point, you're wondering what in the world is going on, that your team seems schizophrenic. I call it organizational psychosis, a condition when thoughts and emotions are impaired and contact with reality appears lost."

"What do I do if that happens?"

"You stay calm," The Catalyst answered. "This is a normal process in any significant transition effort. If you overreact, you won't facilitate Five-Star Change. If you underreact, the same. Think of it as people needing to cross a wobbly footbridge over a canyon. Some are looking at the bridge and chasm below with fear. Others are crossing the bridge with trepidation. At the same time, there are members on the other side, relieved and exhilarated, their adrenaline pumping."

Ben jotted down notes, sketching the bridge metaphor. "That's good," he said. "How do you help people in the ending zone, who haven't crossed the bridge yet?"

"Are you familiar with Kubler-Ross and her stages of grief?"

"I'm not," Ben admitted.

"No worries. Elizabeth Kubler-Ross was an American-Swiss psychiatrist. I lived in Scottsdale when she passed away there, several years ago. She wrote a bestselling book titled, *On Death and Dying*. The interesting thing is that her five stages of grieving reflect what many go through in the process of adopting a new idea. Give me a second." The Catalyst drew on a new sheet of paper.

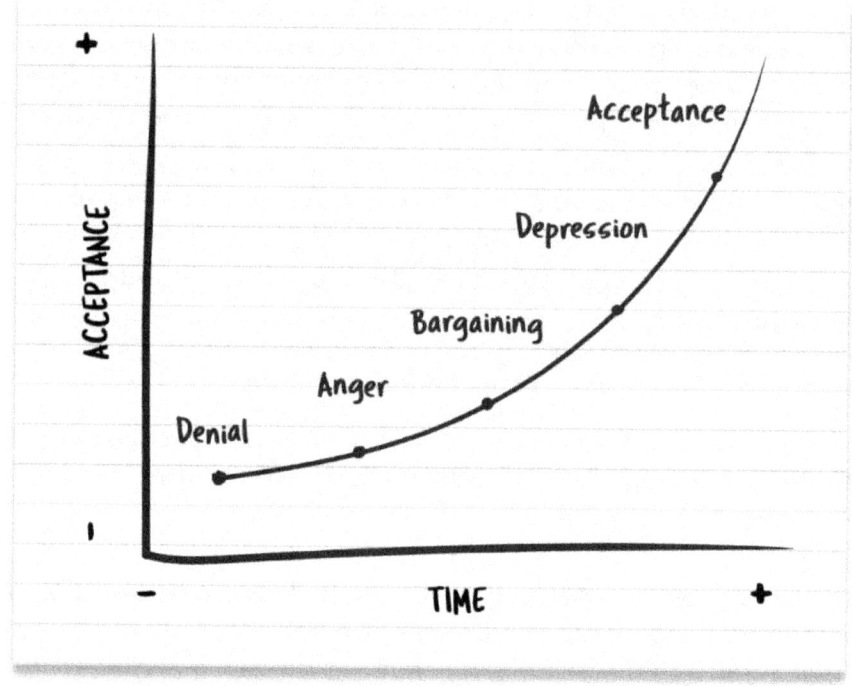

"First there's denial, then anger, followed by bargaining, depression, and acceptance. Depression may be a bit dramatic sounding for organizational change, but sadness or feeling numb are common equivalents. Remember, these emotions happen before acceptance. That's why patience is part of the transition plan, because leaders need to provide space for their people to grieve properly, after announcing a significant innovation. Chances are, when a new thing is implemented, something familiar goes away. It could be relationships, practices, titles, or locations. People need time and understanding as they say 'good-bye' and grieve the loss. Even if the change is considered good, most people need space to let go of status quo."

Ben chuckled. "Oh my gosh, I never thought of it that way. That makes so much sense when I think of how our family and the company have processed changes in the past."

"Good. I'm glad this makes sense." The Catalyst held up the s-curve graphic again. "So that's the dip. It's the most intense portion of the s-curve. After the dip comes point 3. This is where you start to see progress. You're still in a new phase, but you're beginning to get buy-in. Early adopters are accepting the change and you begin seeing results. After stage 3 comes stage 4. In a start-up, it's where you need to implement systems that organize the progress. A lot of flash-in-the-pan dot-com companies die here, because they fail to implement managerial systems."

"That makes sense," Ben said, writing more.

"If you're able to implement systems to stabilize the progress, you'll get to a point where good things are happening. This is point 5, the second most strategic phase in the s-curve."

"Why is this the second most important phase, if everything is going well?"

"It's strategic because people feel happy and leaders experience a sense of relief that their new ideas are paying off. But the danger is resting on your laurels. Leaders feel relieved and perhaps tired, so they want to enjoy the fruit of their hard work. The danger of stage 5 is that the sense of satisfaction tempts us to overlook the need to think of the next new thing, the second s-curve."

The Catalyst lowered his tablet from the webcam and drew on it, then he lifted it up again.

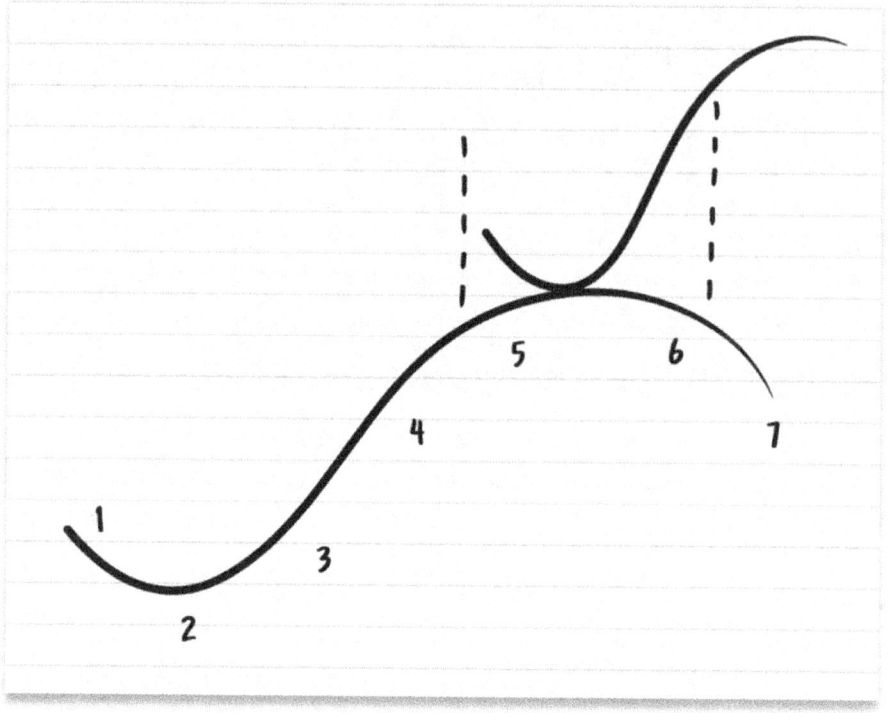

"Stage 5 is where leaders need to be thinking ahead of everyone else, seeing what's around the bend in the road. If you wait too long, enjoying the productivity of your investment, you'll move to stage 6 without realizing it. This is where momentum starts to dissipate and, while not significantly noticeable, decline begins. After stage 6 comes stage 7, when inertia is lost and turn around becomes very difficult, if not impossible. Someone said, 'It's easier to give birth than to resurrect the dead.' Many a company fails because it waits too long to implement significant changes, resulting in death."

"Like Blockbuster, Kmart, Sears, Toys R Us?" Ben reflected.

The Catalyst chuckled. "You get it."

"That's so interesting," Ben responded. "So, you're saying, I need to be thinking about what's next, when our people have adopted the new change and feel good about what's happening."

"Exactly," The Catalyst confirmed.

"That's helpful," Ben responded. "Sorry, but let me go back a bit. What can you give me to help my people get through the dip?"

"The fact that you're asking that question tells me you'll figure it out. There's no recipe or pat answer, but offering encouragement and hope, along with a listening ear, may be all it takes for most of your people to progress. If nothing else, by understanding what's going on in them should help you remain calm, as you keep moving forward. People are looking to you for confidence and reassurance. Kotter suggests planning small wins to feel victorious about progress. Don't just plan on a big celebration at the end."

"That makes sense," Ben responded.

"Ben, I need to run to another meeting, but I wanted to tell you that I think my job is pretty much done. You've gotten the essentials of what creates Five-Star Change."

"I understand. I'm extremely appreciative of your time thus far."

"You're welcome. I've got an idea up my sleeve for a final meeting," The Catalyst remarked.

"What is it?" Ben inquired.

The Catalyst chuckled. "Well, if I told you, you may not want to attend. I'll be in touch."

Meeting Notes:
- Sell the problem to make people hungry for your solution.
- A pilot program is a great way to introduce people to a new idea, allowing them to test drive it and thus remove the fear of unfamiliarity.
- The s-curve reflects a typical evolution of a new company, program or idea.
- All organizations eventually die, but they can prolong themselves with perpetual renewal.
- The 2nd curve or next curve concept involves initiating a change before it's felt by most; leaders need to stay ahead of the curve.
- During the dip in the s-curve, people are prone to experience saying good-bye to old things, hello to new ones, and the disconcerting time between these.
- Grieving conveys the range and sequence of emotions people experience as they move from the past to the future; don't rush or shame good grieving.

chapter ten

A week or so after their video conference, Ben headed for his next meeting with The Catalyst. He drove up the 101, as he had done previously. The consultant's final comment at the end of their last discussion left him curious as to this day's agenda.

Ben exited the freeway on Lindero Canyon Road, just as he did when he met with The Catalyst at the Four Seasons Hotel and The Stonehaus, but this time the address he put into his navigation system took him past the hotel. He crossed the intersection and turned right, through the gates of Valley Oaks Memorial Park, a cemetery. *The Catalyst must have accidentally sent the wrong address*, Ben thought. He turned into the chapel parking lot, so he could look up The Catalyst's number to call him. Just as he put the car into park, he saw the friendly consultant wave, smiling at him from the sidewalk. Ben turned off the car and chuckled to himself as he got out.

"How are you doing, my friend?" The Catalyst asked, approaching Ben with an outstretched hand.

"Well, I was doing well until I turned into this place. Are you trying to tell me something?" Ben said with the laugh. The two men shook hands.

The Catalyst chuckled. "I thought this might make for an interesting last meeting," he said. "You up for a little walk?"

"Sure. Why not?" Ben tucked his notepad and pen under his arm.

The Catalyst pointed up the street, to denote their direction. "Have you thought more since our last meeting, about your Transition Plan?"

"I've thought a lot about it," Ben answered. "I deeply appreciate all the help you've provided. I don't know what I'd have done without your wisdom. More than likely, our plan would be in the two thirds of change initiatives that fail or certainly fall short of Five-Star Change."

"I'm glad our meetings have been valuable to you," The Catalyst said. "I knew you were a fast read. Five-Star Change efforts need strong leaders for them to succeed."

"Thanks. I've written several pages of notes on what we can do, to get the reticent Opinion Leaders to have buy-in, along with adjusting our time, and tweaking how much we want to change in this process. As I mentioned, I've identified and invited our Progressives to help me strategize, so I'm feeling pretty good about the process at this point."

"That's great," The Catalyst confirmed. "I'm confident that you'll lead your upcoming change project valiantly."

As the two men neared the end of the street, The Catalyst pointed to the left, toward two black beach chairs sitting halfway up the green lawn, to the right of a babbling brook water feature.

"What's this?" Ben asked.

"I thought this might be a good place to do some reflection." The two men stood in front of the chairs, sitting between two head stones. "This is my wife's and my future grave site. We're hoping we don't have to use it for a few decades, but one never knows," he said, chuckling. "This grave, to the left, is where Ron Helus is buried. He was the Ventura County Sheriff's Office sergeant who was killed in the Borderline Bar & Grill shootings in 2018, as he defended the patrons."

"Wow, that was a terrible event," Ben whispered, respectfully. "I heard about that."

"Over there, on the other side of the brook, is the actor Tom Selleck's family plot. Up the hill in front of us, in the little mausoleum that says Carpenter, is where Karen Carpenter is entombed. She was a famous singer in my day. So, you can see, we'll be in pretty good company. Please, have a seat," The Catalyst said, pointing to one of the chairs.

The two men sat down, facing toward the Santa Monica Mountains that separate the Conejo Valley from Malibu and the Pacific Ocean. The sounds of the running water and the tranquility of the cemetery provided a peaceful setting, replacing the initial anxiousness Ben felt at talking business in a memorial park.

"You're probably wondering why I asked you to meet me here," The Catalyst said.

"That would be the proverbial elephant in the room," Ben responded, smiling.

"Over the course of my life, I've learned personally and professionally that leaders aren't good at reflecting. They tend to be doers, always looking at the next mountain to climb, the deal on the horizon, the upcoming goal around the corner. But, I see something special in you, Ben. I think you've got a lot of potential, so I want to emphasize the importance of intentional reflection."

"Thanks," Ben said. "What does reflection have to do with Five-Star Change?"

"In my mind, it has a lot to do with it, because when leaders fail to help their people change effectively, they tend to cling to status quo. They fear moving forward, conquering new territories, and thus resist what can make them better."

Ben made notes on his tablet.

"Five-Star Change is obviously about organizational improvement, but it goes much further than that. Change is life. The only stress-less moment in life is death. It's the tension in the violin string that allows it to make music. All change is not good. Some ideas are bad. But good things require us to change, too. When we resist new ideas by nature, we avoid becoming the people we were meant to be and desire to be. We settle for less. Five-Star Change is a life skill, not just a good business practice."

Ben looked up from his notepad. "So, what does my role as a leader in an organization have to do with my people's personal lives, other than employment and making a living?"

"That's my point. Everyone is impacted by organizations, whether as employees or volunteers. Organizations, no matter their mission, must continually change, if they are to survive. That's truer now than at any time in history. So, when organizational leaders employ Five-Star Change practices, they teach and condition their people to get good at adopting new things in general. We can't compartmentalize our lives. Roles and experiences in life influence each other. They overlap."

Ben chuckled quietly. "I guess I've had my nose pretty close to the grindstone."

"Tell me more."

"I mean, I've been thinking about the innovation our division needs. I haven't really been thinking about a bigger picture."

"I grew up on a farm in the Midwest," The Catalyst said, "so perhaps that explains the vernacular of this metaphor. My dad used to say, 'Life is like a roll of toilet paper. The less you have left, the faster it goes.'"

The two men chuckled.

"When I hit midlife, I started investing more of my time teaching young adults at universities and doing research on how to identify and develop leaders while they're moldable, not moldy. Every great leader was at one time a ten-year-old, so how can we get to them while they're pliable in their character, yet elevated in their cognitions? That's why I launched a non-profit organization, committed to identifying and developing future leaders today."

"I guess I'm not at midlife yet, but I certainly understand why that's important," Ben said.

"Here's my point," The Catalyst explained. "Every time a leader implements a flawed transition, he or she conditions those involved to resist change. When this happens over and over, we immunize entire organizations and even society to be suspicious of and resist new ideas, many of which possess the power to improve life, not just make money."

Ben continued writing. "I don't want to fumble this. I think I get it." Ben paused. "So, can I ask you why people call you The Catalyst?"

The consultant chuckled. "I wasn't trying to put you off the first time we met. I honestly don't recall when it began. Someone, somewhere, sometime, identified me as a person who helped others pursue change effectively, so they called me that as a sort of honoring moniker. But it's a bit of an irony because, if you look up the word *catalyst,* one of the definitions is a substance that increases the rate of a chemical reaction without itself undergoing any permanent chemical change. In organizational life, leaders can't stay the same, if they want to help their organizations change. You need to be thinking about what you need to do or how you need to be different, if you want the organization you serve to change. So, in a way, the nickname Catalyst is a bit of a misnomer. I'd encourage you to think about what you'll need to change if you want to embrace this new idea. I believe it was William Bridges who said, 'You can't move on the outside without traveling within.'"

Ben continued writing and then looked up. "Weird as it seemed, I'm glad you set up our meeting here. It changes my perspective."

"Macabre as it may seem, reflecting on our own mortality periodically may not add days to our life, but it adds life to our days. I think I read that in a greeting card somewhere, but it's true nonetheless," The Catalyst said, chuckling. "When we as leaders help people change and improve effectively, we do the same for others. Look at that grave over there." The Catalyst pointed to a dark burgundy, granite headstone nearby. "Look at the date. It says 1940 to 2014. That dash between the year of birth and year of death represents an entire life. What you do in your dash is important."

Ben nodded as he pondered the idea.

The Catalyst continued, "One of the main jobs as parents and leaders is to help people learn how to transition, because it's a major part of living well. That's why leaders who don't understand Five-Star Change, hinder their organizations and the people they employ. Each transition is in and of itself a lesson on living well, not just running a strong company. Improvements are opportunities for us to practice effective transitions. The more we do it well, the better we get at it, and a result is stronger organizations and people."

"I've been pretty nearsighted."

"Good metaphor. Twenty-twenty vision means you see things well up close and at a distance. Visionary leaders do that, helping their people see what needs to be done immediately, while keeping the future in sight. It's a valuable role we serve in society."

The two men talked much more about work, life, family, leadership, and transitions. As they stood to leave, Ben leaned in and hugged his mentor.

"Thank you," he said. "Thank you very much. I can't tell you how much I've appreciated our times together, but especially today's meeting."

"You're more than welcome, my friend," The Catalyst said, patting Ben on the back. "Now it's your turn to pass the baton of Five-Star Change."

And so, he did. The baton is the book you just read.

Meeting Notes:
- Leaders need to make time to reflect, especially when it comes to facilitating transitions.
- Change is life. The only stress-free moment in life is death.
- Leaders need to facilitate Five-Star Change, because their larger responsibility is helping people embrace new ideas and respond to changes throughout life.
- Flawed transition efforts condition people to avoid change, seeing it as bad
- Leaders must ask themselves; What do I need to change myself, if I am to lead change in my organization and among others?

chapter eleven

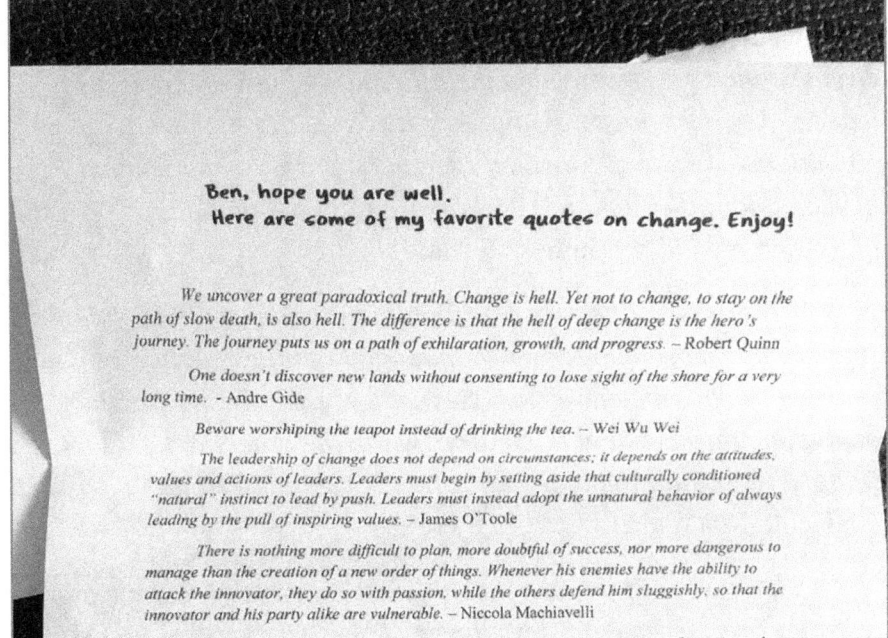

A few weeks after their final meeting, Ben received an envelope in the mail from The Catalyst. It contained printed pages and a handwritten message at the top, "Ben, Hope you are well. Here are some of my favorite quotes on change! Enjoy!"

Ben smiled as he leaned back in his chair and read them.

We uncover a great paradoxical truth. Change is hell. Yet not to change, to stay on the path of slow death, is also hell. The difference is that the hell of deep change is the hero's journey. The journey puts us on a path of exhilaration, growth, and progress. – Robert Quinn

FIVE STAR CHANGE

One does not discover new lands without consenting to lose sight of the shore for a very long time. – Andre Gide

Worshiping the teapot instead of drinking the tea. – Wei Wu Wei

The leadership of change does not depend on circumstances; it depends on the attitudes, values and actions of leaders. Leaders must begin by setting aside that culturally conditioned "natural" instinct to lead by push. Leaders must instead adopt the unnatural behavior of always leading by the pull of inspiring values. – James O'Toole

There is nothing more difficult to plan, more doubtful of success, nor more dangerous to manage than the creation of a new order of things. Whenever his enemies have the ability to attack the innovator, they do so with passion, while the others defend him sluggishly, so that the innovator and his party alike are vulnerable. – Niccolo Machiavelli

Most seek quantum leaps in performance levels by pursuing a strategy of incremental investment. This strategy does not work. The land of excellence is safely guarded from unworthy intruders. At the gates stand two fearsome sentries – risk and learning. The keys to entry are faith and courage. – Robert Quinn

The art of progress is to preserve order amid change and to preserve change amid order. – Alfred North Whitehead

It's not so much that we're afraid of change or so in love with the old ways, but it's that place in between that we fear. It's like being between trapezes. It's Linus when his blanket is in the dryer. There's nothing to hold onto. – Marilyn Ferguson

All changes, even the most longed for, have their melancholy; for what we leave behind is part of ourselves; we must die to one life before we can enter into another. – Anatole France

Great is the art of beginning, but greater the art of ending.
– Henry Wadsworth Longfellow

A friend of ours was a disciple of William Edwards Deming, who did more to bring the era of people-as-cogs to a close than anyone. One evening, at a dinner for Dr. Deming, our friend asked him if he could sum up his entire theory of work, production, statistics, variations, systems, knowledge, and control in a single sentence. Deming did it in two words: "People matter."
– Harvey Robbins and Michael Finley

The present is a time of great entrepreneurial ferment, where old and staid institutions suddenly have to become very limber. The only things that evolve by themselves in an organization are disorder, friction, and malperformance. – Peter Drucker

In Italy, for thirty years under the Borgias, they had warfare, terror, murder, bloodshed. They produced Michelangelo, Leonardo da Vinci, and the Renaissance. In Switzerland they had brotherly love, five hundred years of democracy and peace, and what did they produce? The cuckoo clock. – Orson Welles

An army of sheep led by a lion would defeat an army of lions led by a sheep. – Arab Proverb

He that will not apply new remedies must expect new evils.
– Francis Bacon

If people don't get it, don't fix the people—fix the process.
– W. Edwards Deming

There is much talk of slaying sacred cows. Few are slain; most die of old age. The mandate for change is seldom bold enough to overcome entrenched obstacles to change. – Price Waterhouse Change Integration Team

The world fears a new experience more than it fears anything, because a new experience displaces so many old experiences. The world doesn't fear a new idea. It can pigeon-hole any idea. But it can't pigeon-hole a real new experience. – D. H. Lawrence

If you have always done it that way, it is probably wrong. – Charles Kettering

Confusion is a word we have invented for an order which is not yet understood. – Henry Miller

I don't know the key to success, but the key to failure is trying to please everybody. – Anonymous

For every action, there is an equal and opposite criticism. – Anonymous

An adventure is only an inconvenience rightly understood. An inconvenience is only an adventure wrongly understood. – G. K. Chesterton

It doesn't work to leap a twenty-foot chasm in two ten-foot jumps. – American Proverb

Beginnings are always messy. – John Galsworthy

The world we created today has problems which cannot be solved by thinking the way we thought when we created them. – Albert Einstein

What is to give light, must endure burning. – Viktor Frankl

W. Edwards Deming met with a group of executives and asked, "How many of you have dead wood on your staff?" Most or all of the hands went up. "Did you hire them that way or did you kill them?"

As people in an organization become further removed from being able to influence changes that affect them, their understanding of, commitment to, and ownership of these changes decreases commensurately. – Robert Jacobs

Say the word "change" to any randomly selected group and you will likely get three different types of responses. Some throw up their hands and say, "Not again!" Others throw up their hands and say, "Well, it's about time." The third group will simply throw up. – Anonymous

Life is either a daring adventure or nothing. – Helen Keller

A single rower can easily alter or impede the group's progress simply by resting on the oars. It's the same in organizations. A few people, with no particular malign in their hearts, can prevent good changes from taking place. It is called resistance, or foot-dragging, and it is the veto privilege even the humblest worker can use. – Harvey Robbins and Michael Finley

One of the greatest pains to human nature is the pain of a new idea. It makes you think that after all, your favorite notions may be wrong, your firmest beliefs ill-founded. Naturally, the common person hates a new idea and is disposed more or less to ill-treat the original person who brings it. – Walter Bagehot

Deep change requires more than the identification of the problem and a call for action. It requires looking beyond the scope of the problem and finding the actual source of the trouble. The real problem is frequently located where we would least expect to find it, inside ourselves. Deep change requires an evaluation of the ideologies beyond the organizational culture. – Robert Quinn

The Greek word for repent (meta-noia) literally means to have a "change of mind."

about the author

Alan E. Nelson teaches and has taught leadership, organizational behavior, and organizational change at institutions such as the USC Marshall and UCI Merage business schools, Pepperdine University, and the Naval Postgraduate School. He earned a master's degree in communication-psychology and a doctorate in leadership from the University of San Diego. The NCM mentioned in this book stands for the Nelson Change Model that he's taught in most of his MBA courses. Alan has authored over 30 books and 200 articles on leadership and personal growth themes. At midlife, he decided to focus on identifying and developing leaders while they're moldable, not moldy. He founded KidLead Inc., a non-profit, and LeadYoung Training Systems, designing international training curricula for 3- to 23-year-olds.

Alan has been married for nearly 40 years to Nancy, who was hired as a 25-year-old by John C. Maxwell, renowned pastor, speaker, author, and leadership expert, to be on his leadership team. She is now an executive director in senior living. The Nelsons have three grown sons and, as of this book, two granddaughters. They live north of Los Angeles in Thousand Oaks, California. The Nelsons enjoy movies, eating out, Zooming with Juniper and Ivy, and walks along the beach in nearby Malibu and Santa Barbara.

For information on Dr. Nelson's training and speaking, go to www.AlanENelson.com or to LinkedIn at http://www.linkedin/in/alanenelson/. You can email the author at dralanenelson@gmail.com.

This book offers a broad array of practical tools for new managers to understand how their organization behaves as well as offering leadership to their teams. This is a must read for those who are put in charge of others.

Dealing with difficult people and succeeding with others requires knowledge of what makes people tick. The bottom line is understanding that everyone seeks honor, to be valued.

A reader-friendly book on Dr. Nelson's work since midlife, on identifying and developing leadership talent early, getting to leaders while they're moldable, not moldy. This landmark book offers practical advice for parents and those who work with young leaders, ages 3-23.

www.ingramcontent.com/pod-product-compliance
Lightning Source LLC
Chambersburg PA
CBHW070805220526
45466CB00002B/556